How I Met Prince Charming

BY

Etonde Akamangwa

How I Met Prince Charming Print Edition
ISBN 13: 978-1985766921
Copyright © 2018 Etonde Akamangwa

Contents

Dedication

To the Prince of Peace, my Lord Jesus Christ. Your praise will continuously be on my lips as I recite my composition concerning my King. You have dealt bountifully toward me. My life is a testimony of your goodness toward all races.

To my parents: Francis Achiri Ade (Dad), who slept in The Lord in 2015. You will always be my daddy. Your words are engraved in my heart forever, and my memories with you will last a lifetime. Thank you for your letter which taught me what it takes to stay married. It is a treasure that will be passed down to my kids. Thank you for being the best daddy in the world.

To Rose Ade (Mom), thank you for teaching me all you know about marriage. Thank you for sticking with Daddy for 38 years until his death.

Acknowledgements

My loving husband, Linus Akamangwa: God gave me you. Thank you for loving me regardless of my shortcomings. Our journey of love is just starting, and God will take us places beyond our imagination as we continue to seek Him first in all we do.

My daughters, Njuamboh and Ngeniform: I love you and will always be your mommy. My prayer is for you girls to experience the love of God and share His goodness to the world.

Kay Gramm, thank you for standing with me in prayer and for all the wisdom you poured into my life.

Jacky Lacher, thank you for listening to me and letting me know my husband is not the enemy.

Cyndy Leamon, thank you for being an example and pointing me to the Word.

To all the other Titus 2 women not mentioned here, I say thank you for pouring into the lives of young mothers.

Introduction

You may have picked up this book for several different reasons. Perhaps you are married, and you need insights on how to manage the storms of life. Maybe you are trying to make sense of why marriage takes so much effort to keep it going. Perhaps you are still looking forward to being married, and you just want to read about how I met my Prince Charming. Or, maybe you have gone through a divorce, and you are hurting and can't move on. You may know someone who is struggling with their marriage, and you are looking for ways to help them.

Can marriage be great? Can we actually be happy for a lifetime with one spouse? What is this love thing anyway? Why are many marriages failing if love does not fail? Are we missing something about love?

This book might not answer all these questions on marriage, but it will show you how my walk with God answered many of them, including the main one: "Is happily ever after a reality or a hoax?"

I will also take you through my adventure of love with my spouse. We were the perfect couple on the outside but could not communicate in peace. You will see the struggles and storms of life we faced and how God revealed His truth to us.

Also included is a letter from my dad, which contains so much wisdom about marriage. At the end, I share that love has already been done. We don't have to perform because Jesus has already accomplished love. All we need is to allow Jesus to manifest His life through us. We can't do marriage in our own strength.

"In this the love of God was manifested toward us, that God has sent His only begotten Son into the world, that we might live through Him."
- 1 John 4:9 NKJV

www.victorynowmin.org

Chapter One

Reality or Hoax?

I was 16 years old when my entire family had our eyes fixed on the live CNN broadcast of the funeral of Diana, Princess of Wales on September 6th, 1997. I could not stop the tears rolling freely down my cheeks as we watched from our home in Cameroon, West Africa.

My heart was broken by her fantasy story gone terribly wrong. I felt lost and confused about the concept of happily-ever-after in marriages. If this real-life princess didn't experience her own fairytale ending, what hope did I have?

Then I realized that I wasn't the only one watching, but around 2.5 billion other people worldwide joined me, as well. The entire world had come to a halt. Not only did the British people mourn, we all grieved as we watched the roughly four-mile processional carry the casket of the 36-year-old beautiful, elegant, and strong Royal through the streets of central London. The "People's Princess" had died in the prime of her life.

Lady Diana met Prince Charles when she was only 16 and he was 29, and the British people were given a national holiday to watch their fairytale wedding on July 29, 1981. I remember my dad telling me, "That was the wedding of the century."

Every girl of 16 dreams of living as a princess in Buckingham Palace, which is one of the only monarchies that reveals a picture of what royal living looks like. It seemed she was living the fairytale dream life of every girl! However, in reality it was not a fairytale at all: Princess Diana and Prince Charles were divorced a year prior to her tragic death. She died on August 31, 1997 in a car crash at the Pont de l'Alma road tunnel in Paris, France with her boyfriend Dodi Fayed.

The royal divorce was worldwide breaking TV news and made the headlines of every newspaper. This not-so-fairy-tale ending left the world in shock:

mourning and confused.

Why would a princess divorce Buckingham Palace, and publicly take off her crown and walk away? Who would reject the royal lifestyle with every luxury and privilege: everything at her service? What happened to the happily-ever-after for Princess Diana and Prince Charles?

Was this a 20th Century royal hoax on display?

You have likely heard this passage read at a wedding, or maybe even at your own wedding: "Love never fails" (1 Corinthians 13:8). I also hear a lot of people use the phrase, "Let love lead." Well, if love never fails, and if love leads, why do we see many marriages failing? Why are there many broken-hearted people around us looking and searching for love? If the Bible is true -- which I personally know without a doubt that the Bible is the absolute truth – what are we missing?

Have we missed this love thing completely? Is there something hidden in the pages of scripture that has yet to be revealed about love?

Hollywood has painted an image in the minds of our children about meeting Prince Charming and living happily ever after. Yet, the same producers and actors seem to be searching for love by marrying, and remarrying, nonstop. Many, on the other hand, have decided not to even give marriage a try for fear of being hurt.

Is it even worth it to marry anymore? Is marriage a set up? Can marriage last a lifetime and still be enjoyable? Can you actually have a great marriage? What is mankind searching for in the name of love? Well, come with me on this adventure called love as we seek answers to these questions.

When Our Walls Came Crumbling Down

Someone told me the other day that my husband and I are a good-looking couple. Another said that there is "something" about us when we walk into a room. A pastor we met for the very first time in 2014 prophesied to us that our union was a divine connection. Words!!!!! Little did they know that these statements would take me down memory lane – to a time when our walls (almost) came crumbling down.

I remember very well that Sunday morning, in the spring of 2010, in South Bend, Indiana; it was one of our darkest days. It was finally getting warm outside and the winter coats were gradually being put away. It was the perfect morning to put on bright and beautiful colors to wear to church. Sunday mornings are usually hectic if you have little kids, and the rush to be out of the house on time for church can easily result in many frustrations.

The drive to church would sometimes be extremely quiet because we were not talking to each other. Or, on the contrary, very loud from a screaming kid! During the baby shower of our first daughter, one of our very good friends told us that kids are a blessing, but they can be very challenging in your marriage relationship. How true this was.

Our attitude toward kids as a blessing is very important in how we relate with them. (Thanks Jeff!) As parents, we must be intentional about making our homes secure and free of strife. Children watch our actions, and they are very likely to become who they see. Strongholds formed at home start building walls in kids that will affect their future relationships.

As PARENTS, WE MUST BE INTENTIONAL ABOUT MAKING OUR HOMES SECURE AND FREE OF STRIFE.

In our home, that beautiful spring Sunday was one of the turning points in our marriage. We were less than three years into our relationship and had been married less than two. Our oldest daughter was about six months old, and on the outside, we were the perfect couple: a young, growing family living in a beautiful home, in an upper-middle-class neighborhood, with well-manicured green lawns displaying beautiful hanging spring flowers.

Driving expensive luxury cars was our norm. In fact, my husband's gift to himself, for finishing medical residency, was a brand-new Mercedes S550 – fresh off the show room floor – which he paid off within a year. For our baby shower, he gave me a Porsche Cayenne S-Class. We also had a great church family that loved us dearly. What more could one ask for?

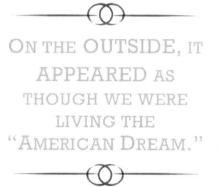

ON THE OUTSIDE, IT APPEARED AS THOUGH WE WERE LIVING THE "AMERICAN DREAM."

It was the dream life to many onlookers – an educated, hard-working, African migrant family that had the American dream working well for them.

Others envied our life, yet at breakfast before church that Sunday, my husband looked me straight in the eyes and said, "What is the reason for us to look perfect on the outside and can hardly stand each other at home? Why should we go to church anyway?"

aa   Well, even though there were signs, I did not see this coming! There was a lot of buildup of strife in our home and we were not communicating well. Our intimacy was out the door, especially with a baby. We quarreled over almost everything: parenting techniques, who had to wash the car, food prep-

WE WERE AT A POINT IN OUR MARRIAGE WHERE WE NEEDED DIVINE INTERVENTION!

aration, changing diapers, even who went to the store with the baby. You name it – we disagreed!

Oh, the struggles new parents go through! Before having kids, I used to always wonder why parents with toddlers went their separate ways, yet now it was almost becoming my own reality. Separation was knocking at our door. Neither me, nor my husband, wanted to respect or submit to the other; neither of us would admit to being wrong.

In my eyes, I was doing all I knew to do and was getting no appreciation or affirmation in return. From his perspective, he was working very hard to provide for us and was not getting any respect. I remember responding that morning to his crushing remark, "That is the very reason we need to be in church."

Why am I telling you this story? I want to show

you that we had gotten to a point in our marriage where we needed **divine intervention**. We had given marriage our all but had failed. Our natural strength and knowledge were not enough to build, and sustain, our home. We ran out of love in the midst of building our family. We had come to the end of ourselves. Although we had everything the world called success, we struggled with our marriage to the point of being tempted to quit.

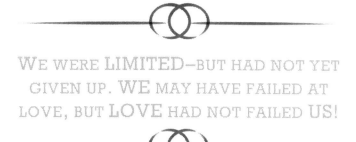

WE WERE LIMITED–BUT HAD NOT YET
GIVEN UP. WE MAY HAVE FAILED AT
LOVE, BUT LOVE HAD NOT FAILED US!

Sure, we were Christians, but God was not our source. It was all just about making a name for ourselves. Yet, I wanted to make my marriage work. I did not want my daughter to be a statistic. I was determined to see that she grew up with both parents in the home and that it would be stable and peaceful; our little girl would not see us throwing curse words at each other and arguing.

I searched for help because we needed it! My soul wanted more, and I was certain that God would not ever let me down. God was the one who had told me to marry my husband, so I went back to my source of life. What the Holy Spirit revealed to me is what saved my marriage, and I will explain more in detail in another chapter, so keep reading!

You may be at this same point in your marriage and need help. Stop trying to fake your life away when you can reach out and receive help. Your Heavenly Father loves you and wants the best for your marriage. There is hope! I knew this, so I reached out to my pastor and made an appointment to see him. Little did I know what was coming!

Okay, just to let you know, it's not an African thing for a man to humble himself and go for counseling; or maybe most men, regardless of their culture, hate counseling in general. Regardless, in our African culture, the woman is always considered to be the one who is at fault. In most cases, even when African women reach out to their own parents for help, their families will support the man.

Yet, my husband chose to seek help, rather than allow pride to destroy our family! As I mentioned before, seeking counseling is not usually done in our culture; the men have it all figured out, and simply do things their own way and not God's way. I bless God for my husband who decided to humble himself before God, broke the cultural stereotype, and allowed God to restore our family.

"My brothers, humble yourselves! Your marriages can be better than what you are going through right now. I got tired of my mediocre marriage. I knew in my heart that my marriage could be better. So, I went for counseling and it helped. I cried out to God for help, and He restored my marriage. God also wants to restore <u>your</u> marriage. If we can't be successful at home, we have failed. Successfully leading our families – our wives and children – is our priority."

– Linus Akamangwa

If you have never been to marriage counseling, this is how it goes: the couple talks, and the pastor just listens. Each spouse is given a chance to talk without the other interrupting. A lot of couples usually argue during the counseling sessions, but at least in our case we could communicate without fighting.

A good Pastor counsels at the end based on what he hears from both sides. After my husband spoke, a weight was lifted from us. We realized we both had come into the marriage with lots of baggage – strongholds and wounds from the past that had built walls in us that needed to be torn down and put yokes on us that needed to be broken.

Neither of us were directly responsible for these strongholds, but it was vital that we help each other overcome them. We had to become sensitive to each other's triggers. One word from me could open up an old wound of my husband's, and vice versa. Not only this, but we later learned that even though our marriage was at war, we were not enemies!

However, there is an enemy that seeks to steal, to kill, and to destroy our marriages. The devil was roaming about – like a roaring lion – seeking to devour our family (1 Peter 5:8). What an eye opener this was to us! We were determined to fight as one for our marriage – in unity and in agreement for our good.

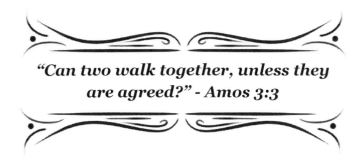

"Can two walk together, unless they are agreed?" - Amos 3:3

I remember getting on my knees and asking

God for help. I knew I could not use my own wisdom. I asked God, "Show me Lord where I'm going wrong, and teach me how to be a better wife to my husband and mother to our daughters."

God did a heart surgery on me; it felt like a heart transplant even though I was already born-again. He

THE CHANGE YOU NEED STARTS WITH YOU AND THE HOLY SPIRIT.

gives us a new heart when we first come to Christ, but the world – and circumstances – had stained my heart. Past hurts had hardened my heart toward my husband, so I needed healing. I had to let go and let the Holy Spirit take charge so that He could work through me.

The change we needed had to start with me, and in me. I had to put on the faithful eyes of compassion, be intentional and stay patient. This process takes time, endurance, and the understanding that only The Holy Spirit can change the hearts of men. Too often, we as women try to help the Holy Spirit. He is our helper and comforter, but not vice versa! We end up doing very badly in our attempts to do His job because we act in the flesh.

The Holy Spirit had to pull out the unwanted

thorns – the cares of this life – that were choking the life out of me. I had to completely surrender my marriage to the Lord. My husband belongs to the Lord anyway. He is part of the brethren. My children are a gift from God, and I had to hand them back to Him. I needed God to hold my hand and help me.

The meeting with our pastor was the first of many counseling sessions and marriage seminars. Now we are intentional about attending at least two Christian marriage seminars each year. You don't have to wait to be in a crisis to seek counseling!

Couples need maintenance therapy. We listen to teachings on marriage, and, most importantly, seek God for direction. Our victory in marriage over the years has been because of the many lessons we have learned from God.

We learned to die to self and serve each other as unto The Lord. We had to first enter into relationship with God on a personal level; our first marriage is with Christ and then with each other. The Holy Spirit is our counselor and helper every step of the way. He is the invisible third person

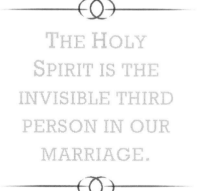

THE HOLY SPIRIT IS THE INVISIBLE THIRD PERSON IN OUR MARRIAGE.

in our marriage – the life-giving power source for the relationship. We serve each other out of our relationship with the Holy Spirit – out of the abundance and overflow of His love in our hearts.

Christ Jesus restored, redeemed and perfected our marriage inwardly, so what you see outwardly is the result of an inward creative work the Word of God has done in our hearts. He pulled us out of the world's darkness and into His marvelous light. When storms come, we now fix our eyes united on Jesus instead of on ourselves.

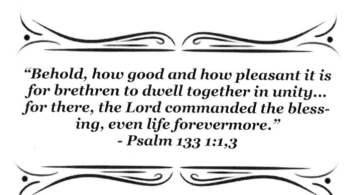

"Behold, how good and how pleasant it is for brethren to dwell together in unity... for there, the Lord commanded the bless-ing, even life forevermore."
- Psalm 133 1:1,3

Our prayer is for other couples to also turn to The Holy Spirit for help and counsel in their marriages. Do not be fooled: you can't have a successful marriage in your own strength. You can't take God out of your "Love Equation." Man + Woman = Baby is not enough. We are made in His image – His likeness

– so God must be included. A successful "Love Equation" is **GOD** + Man + Woman = Baby.

This is a spiritual condition: God ordained the first marriage and He should be a part of your union. You can't look to each other for happiness. God Almighty is the source of eternal joy, so your relationship with God alone is what should keep you happy.

Marriage is not a substitute for a relationship with God. You function as a unit in marriage because God sees you as one. The power of God is released when there is unity and agreement!

So, Marriage is intentional work. It takes dying to self and serving one another out of the love of God that has been shed abroad in our hearts by the Holy Spirit (Romans 5:5).

Marriage on earth should be a reflection of Christ and His Bride – the Church. It is impossible to

"But seek ye first the kingdom of God, and His righteousness; and all these things shall be added unto you."
- Matthew 6:33

have a victorious marriage without God's kind of love (Ephesians 5:32).

There is no love without God! God is love. Your identity in your marriage should never come from what you own. Things will never satisfy your soul (1 John 4:8, Mark 8:36).

Our identities should be found in Christ alone.

www.victorynowmin.org

Chapter Two

My Walk with God

Why would God care about a little African girl from a family of thirteen children? Africa may seem very far away to many of you, but Africa is not far from God! It does not matter how far away your continent may seem to others, it is not far from God. He cares about every human born on earth. Is He not the giver of all life? Your knowledge of His constant presence will change your perspective and how you relate to Him.

That little girl was me. Though I did not understand much as a child, He revealed Himself to me and

I developed a relationship with the Living God who speaks to His children. This same relationship is available to all who believe in His Son, Jesus Christ.

"For God so loved the world that he gave His only begotten Son that whomsoever believes in Him should not perish but have everlasting life. For God did not send His Son into the world to condemn the world, but that the world through Him might be saved. He who believes in Him is not condemned; but he who does not believe is condemned already, because he has not believed in the name of the only begotten Son of God. And this is the condemnation, that the light has come into the world, and men loved darkness rather than light, because their deeds were evil."
- John 3:16-20

The love of God is for the whole world. He speaks to everyone on the face of planet Earth; so, all are without excuse (Romans 1:20). It does not matter how remote or primitive your country is, Jesus died for your sake. Although first world countries may label your continent, and condemn it, what stands is what Jesus did for you. He did not come to condemn the world, but that the world may be saved through Him.

Do you agree that Jesus is the Son of God?

I grew up in a very large family with Christian parents. Church was the norm on Sundays, and my dad used to wake us up as early as five o'clock in the morning to teach us about the Bible. I confessed Jesus as Lord and Savior at age eight at a Young Presbyterian meeting. The youth pastor was Pentecostal and told us about Heaven and why we had to be part of that Kingdom. Based on what he told us, Hell did not sound like a happy place. I'd rather be in a happy and beautiful place – what about you?

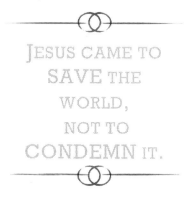

JESUS CAME TO SAVE THE WORLD, NOT TO CONDEMN IT.

There was a significant change in my life the moment I said, "Yes," to Jesus. God started speaking to me, and I could hear Him more clearly. I started to know things about people that no one had told me. I began to have visions of things that eventually came to pass. I didn't know how to explain these things to my family, because I didn't yet understand the gifts of the Spirit, so they even began to hide things from me!

I also had a strong desire to study the Word like never before. My dad encouraged me to read the book of Proverbs, which helped shape my life. I learned to take the wisdom that I found in that book and apply it to everyday situations. Although I was certainly not perfect, it did guide my behavior, and I saw many positive effects in my life. I encourage you to do the same!

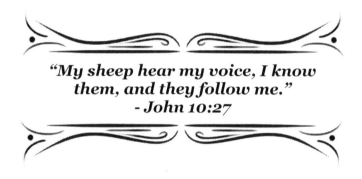

"My sheep hear my voice, I know them, and they follow me."
- John 10:27

Hearing the voice of God clearly – yet wanting to do otherwise – was the biggest challenge I had ever faced. I wanted to do the things my friends were doing, but His voice was constantly speaking truth to my soul. This made me restless, and I struggled with the desires of the flesh.

My point is that I was familiar with God's voice at a very young age. He began to direct me, and although I couldn't explain it to my family or friends, the one thing I knew for sure was that I could communicate with God and we had a real relationship. I could hear His voice, even as I wrestled with my flesh.

Chapter Three

How I Met My Prince

everyone has a story of how they met their Prince Charming. If you have not yet met yours, you will also have a story – although, remember my encouragement to enter into fellowship with God first! One romance may be more exciting than another, or perhaps more awkward! So, let me give you the opportunity to be the judge of my own tale as I take you along the journey of how I met **my** Prince Charming.

Ever since I was a little girl, I wondered who my Prince Charming would be. Who would I live my happily ever after with? What would my children look like? Would they look like me or their dad? I had a mental image of him in my mind: tall, handsome, and with a chocolate complexion just like my daddy. It's okay for a girl to dream, right? This mental image helped me eliminate a lot of people!

Little did I know that the Holy Spirit would remind me of this years later.

My fairy tale started in January, in South Bend, Indiana. For those of you who don't know, January is the coldest, snowiest, iciest month of the year. It is exactly as the weather forecaster always says, "If you have no reason to be outside, stay indoors."

As I sat alone in my empty student apartment, on a typically frigid day, January 30th, 2007, I could almost hear the echoes of my breath. January 30th is always a big deal in my little world. I waited with hope and expectation of receiving a call from my parents, and siblings, who remembered to wish me well on my birthday. And, yes, when my dad remembered, he would usually sing for me. Oh, what special memories I now cherish!

For several years, I had made it a habit to journal important events in my life – specifically for looking back on them with a thankful heart. In reflecting on what I had written, I could see where I had come from as well as where God had taken me from there.

On my 26th birthday, I decided to take a different approach to my journaling. I was single and tired of long distance, over the phone dating. Good luck to all involved in those kinds of emotional, heart-wrecking dating experiences! As I started pouring my heart out in my journal, there was one thing I wanted: to be married. I was ready to settle down. It wasn't due to any pressure from my parents, nor did my friends getting married before me make me feel in a rush to do the same.

Before this, I never had peace to settle down with anyone I had dated. Where there is no peace,

"Grace and peace be multiplied to you in the knowledge of God and of Jesus our Lord, as His divine power has given to us all things that pertain to life and godliness, through the knowledge of Him who called us by glory and virtue, by which have been given to us exceedingly great and precious promises, that through these you may be partakers of the divine nature, having escaped the corruption that is in the world through lust."
- 2 Peter 1:2-4 NKJV

the grace of God is absent. It is very important to follow the peace of God in every decision you make (Colossians 3:15). Only Jesus gives peace; apart from Him there is no peace. Jesus is the Prince of Peace and that is exactly what I needed as I searched for my prince.

Many ladies, as well as gentlemen, forget to consult the Prince of Peace in the search for their prince or princess. You don't want to settle with a prince who has not yet made the Prince of Peace their Lord and Savior. He is the model of what a prince should be. It is the life of the Prince of Peace that is manifested in marriage, so in order to have peace in your marriage, you must get Jesus involved in your search. There will be no peace in your marriage without the Prince of Peace.

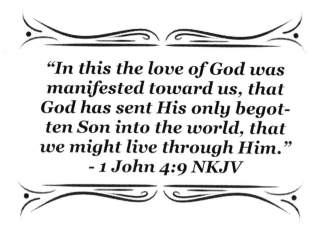

"In this the love of God was manifested toward us, that God has sent His only begotten Son into the world, that we might live through Him."
- 1 John 4:9 NKJV

In my mind, I knew what I wanted. I was not going to compromise my values, so it didn't take me long after a conversation with a guy to know their heart level. It was easy to make a "date funeral" and move on after just one conversation. Some of you reading this

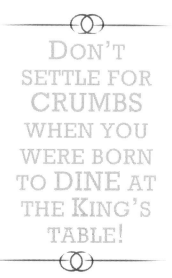

DON'T SETTLE FOR CRUMBS WHEN YOU WERE BORN TO DINE AT THE KING'S TABLE!

need to move on from your current wrecked relationships. Pick a day and plan the emotional funeral; that day can be today! Why wait? You are royalty and need to be treated accordingly. Every princess has access to the very best the King has to offer; don't settle for crumbs when you were born to dine at the King's table with the Prince of Peace. You were born to reign in a Kingdom that cannot be shaken.

As I journaled that day on my twenty-sixth birthday, I came up with a list of twenty-six things I wanted in a husband. Now, this was in addition to the mental picture I had on the physical appearance I was expecting. I know many of you have done the same thing. I was now going into deeper things, not realizing I was limiting God with my list.

<u>My List</u>

1. He should be God fearing
2. Respects humans
3. Loving and cheerful
4. Hard working and positive
5. Open to changes
6. Loves quiet time
7. Encouraging and honest
8. Handsome and taller than me
9. From my country if possible and preferably black. I am open to all races, but he must be willing to settle in Cameroon, West Africa.
10. Loves himself
11. Loves his mom and siblings
12. Loves children
13. Welcoming to strangers
14. Has a giving spirit
15. Loves his future wife and children
16. Loves to travel
17. Loves to dance
18. Romantic
19. Loves to eat healthy
20. Loves sports
21. Cherishes my hard work
22. Tells me he loves from his heart
23. Loves to dress up well
24. Loves to babysit
25. Loves to clean
26. Wants to be married to me forever

But, as I mentioned, too often, we limit God with our lists. I was in for a surprise!

At the top of the list I wrote, "A man who fears The Lord!" This was the key focal point, and it helped me in knowing what to look and listen for. Then, I told

ENJOY YOUR
PERSONAL
RELATIONSHIP
WITH THE
FATHER.

God to take over the search because I was not going to worry about it. Did He not tell us to cast our burdens on Him (1 Peter 5:7)? Why should I worry when He told me to worry not? (Matthew 6:25, 31, 34) In the meantime, I enjoyed my personal relationship with the Father. I was not needy or in lack. I rested in Him because I trusted Him.

That birthday, with my journal, was just the beginning. Now let's fast forward to August 2007. I had traveled to Boston to attend a friend's graduation. Any of my friends and family know that I love to work and help. My friends were like family to me anyway. Is this not what friends do: help and support one another?

You may recall that, from my childhood, I was used to the voice of the Holy Spirit telling me things. It was normal for me to discern His voice. Now, hearing His voice is one thing, but acting on it can be a wrestling match if it is not what we want.

How often do you try to lead the Holy Spirit and

play the Shepherd, rather than the other way around? We often think we can handle things better than He can. The truth is, God knows what is best for us. We have the choice to agree with Him or reject what He offers; He will not force His promises on us. He is a gentle Spirit. The Prince of Peace is a gentleman.

GOD WILL NOT FORCE HIS PROMISES ON US.

A gentleman has these characteristics: love, joy, peace, long-suffering, kindness, goodness, faithfulness, gentleness and self-control. Yes! This is the fruit of the Spirit, and all who are born of God have these same qualities in their new man, in Christ. The love of God has been shed abroad in a gentleman's heart by the Holy Spirit (Galatians 5:22-25, Romans 5:5).

Wash His Feet

As we cooked, cleaned and organized the house for my friend's graduation reception, her uncle helped with moving the heavy stuff around. After a busy afternoon of organization, we all sat at the table to eat and relax. My spoon fell under the table. As I leaned under the table and reached for it, my eyes noticed some ashy feet that needed washing!

All of a sudden, I heard the familiar voice of the Holy Spirit say, **"Wash his feet."** You know, God has a sense of humor, without a doubt. You should have seen the look on my face under that table. *Lord have mercy on your daughter!*

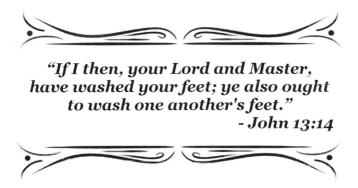

"If I then, your Lord and Master, have washed your feet; ye also ought to wash one another's feet."
- John 13:14

Ding, ding, ding! The wrestling match with God had begun! My soul argued with God, "No, no, no, no! God, You **must** be joking! I'm not going to wash his feet. Besides, he is not even in my age bracket, plus he already has a child! Oh, no, God! This is not him! I did not come here looking for a husband."

I could see God standing and laughing at me. **"You told me to help you. Trust in Me, and I will teach you what love is. I AM love!"**

Seriously, God!?

He gave me a word, and I rebelled right away. Has the Holy Spirit ever given you a word this clear and you just tossed it away? It came when I did not expect it. I had completely forgotten I had told Him to help me with the search for my prince. I did not see anyone around that suited my list. I was in shock mode! Even more, I was sad because I knew it was God. It was the Shepherd's voice that had been speaking to me ever since I was eight years old. I wondered, *What am I supposed to do now?*

THE HOLY SPIRIT HAD EVERYTHING PLANNED OUT!

From this point on, I distanced myself from "Uncle" during the party. I really did not want to have anything to do with him; I purposely talked less to everyone else as well to avoid unwanted attention. Little did I know, the Holy Spirit had everything already planned out!

The next day, after the party, I needed to visit some of my relatives who lived an hour away. Well, guess who volunteered to drive me to see my family? Yes! "Uncle" was the only one who was willing, and available, to take me. *This is awkward!*

I could literally see God smiling at me, **"Etonde, it is okay! Do not be afraid, I AM with you; I will never leave you nor forsake you. I've got this, child!"**

As we drove away, I was silent, timid, and nervous, yet trying to be calm. So, the question came:

"What type of music would you like to listen to?"

"Gospel!" I enthusiastically requested.

"Woooow! Gospel music?" he replied. "You don't find many ladies your age listening to gospel music. I have one in here. It's Joel Osteen's worship band."

"…You know Joel Osteen? I fall asleep listening to the Lakewood worship band every night!"

This immediately turned off the silence switch in the car, as I got excited that we had something in common. We talked about how encouraging Joel's messages were and the impact he had on each of us. The one-hour drive, that I had been dreading, felt like ten minutes!

Seriously, God!

The Holy Spirit is something else. He knows what we like more than we do. He broke the ice between us and made the drive easy and relaxed. He brought His peace in the midst of my nervous-

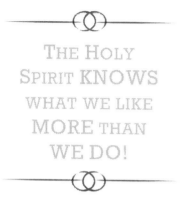

THE HOLY SPIRIT KNOWS WHAT WE LIKE MORE THAN WE DO!

ness. Surely, He is the Prince of Peace. During that drive, our focus was redirected to Him, instead of ourselves. Any time we focus more on God and acknowledge His goodness in our lives rather than ourselves, He always takes the glory. It is the goodness of God that brings all of us to repentance (Romans 2:4).

The interesting part was, when we got to my relatives' home, everyone suspected we had something going on. Now, this actually got me ticked off because no one believed he was just giving me a ride! Regardless, I was not going to argue with anyone on this; maybe it was simply a confirmation.

On our return drive, "Uncle" asked me if I would be interested in visiting him in October in New York, and Joel Osteen was having a concert at Madison Square Garden with his worship band. This just so happened to be during a week-long break I had from school. That was our first date. Joel became the point of focus in most of our discussions, and we shared his messages with each other.

He asked for my number before I left for Indiana. Three months down the road, he asked me to marry him, and six months later we began our marriage journey. (We actually had several wedding dates due both to our Cameroonian culture and migrant paper issues!)

Our steps are surely guided by the Lord, and when we are sensitive to Him we will be in the right place at the right time.

If you are still looking for your prince – or princess – I pray this story encourages you. He or she may not come in the perfect form that your dreams, expectancies, and utopian list describes! Thankfully, our faith in Christ was our focus, rather than our lists.

Yes, have a standard, but be willing to be flexible. The best gifts never come in prettily packaged boxes; Jesus, our Eternal Rock, was born in a stable! He was not the warrior king the Jews were expecting to come in chariots to defeat and

ALLOW CHRIST TO BE YOUR FOCUS, RATHER THAN YOUR LIST!

overthrow the Romans. He was humble and lowly, yet still the Savior of the world. He is the Prince of Peace and our Deliverer – the firstborn Prince who laid down His life for the world. He is our first husband!

For those of you who are already married, and wanting your spouse to change, you have to accept the truth that we can't change another person. (Although, we ladies certainly can sometimes help our men change their clothes!) The only person you can truly change is you. You are the change your marriage needs, so be the change! Your spouse will notice the change in your good actions and positive attitudes toward him or her. Remember, it is the goodness of God that draws men unto repentance (Romans 2:4).

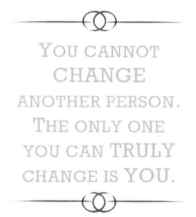

YOU CANNOT CHANGE ANOTHER PERSON. THE ONLY ONE YOU CAN TRULY CHANGE IS YOU.

It is the Holy Spirit Who changes the hearts of men. Wash his or her feet with the love of God shed abroad in your heart by the Holy Spirit. Marriage is service to each other.

And, yes! I went out and bought a home pedicure set. The first time he visited me, I offered to wash his feet; I cut his toe nails and gave those once ashy feet a complete makeover. He never forgets, and I still wash his feet whenever I get the chance.

Each day is a blessing as we go through both the good times and the challenges life throws at us. With Christ at the helm, we are victorious in Him who called us into His service.

As for my list? He actually exceeded my dream list when he brought my husband. He is a God that does exceedingly abundantly above what we ask or think!

"Let the husband render unto the wife due benevolence: and likewise also the wife unto the husband. But he that is married careth for the things that are of the world, how he may please his wife...but she that is married careth for the things of the world, how she may please her husband."
- 1 Corinthians 7:3, 33-34

Chapter Four

The Struggling Bride

Just because the Holy Spirit was involved in picking my prince does not mean I had everything figured out. I had no clue what I was getting myself into – what I was committing to. Marriage to me was more of an imitation rather than a revelation. It felt like a set up – like a burden choking the life out of me.

We started our marriage with a lot of unrealistic expectations. Maybe we had watched too many movies! My parents modeled to me what they knew best, and they were amazing, law-abiding parents. How-

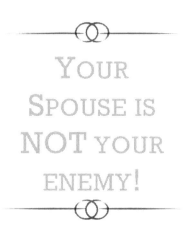

YOUR
SPOUSE IS
NOT YOUR
ENEMY!

ever, they didn't communicate very well and would argue with each other! So, although they were wonderful, I was certain I wanted more than even their example. I wanted my home to be a very peaceful environment.

What brought peace during the first years of our marriage was the word the Holy Spirit gave me, **"I will teach you what love is! I AM love!"** Listen to me, the enemy was after us; he was doing everything possible to destroy our marriage. He might be doing the same in yours right now. Please note: your spouse is not your enemy!

Your Marriage is at War

IT IS
UNREALISTIC
TO MAKE YOUR
SPOUSE THE
SOURCE OF
YOUR
HAPPINESS.

What if Cinderella and Prince Charming knew, as they danced away, their source of happiness would not be found in each other? Wouldn't they be better equipped for battle if they were warned of the ways their marriage would be attacked before they rode away?

What if they were told that their relationship with each other flowed from the overflow of intimacy with the Prince of Peace? If only they were taught that peace in their home would only start the moment they exalted Jesus Christ above their struggles. It is unrealistic to make each other the source of happiness and joy.

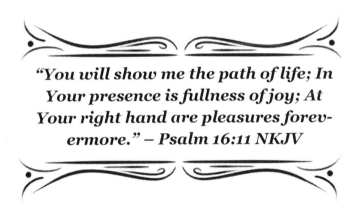

"You will show me the path of life; In Your presence is fullness of joy; At Your right hand are pleasures forevermore." – Psalm 16:11 NKJV

When we look around us, we see broken marriages and hurting children in a society full of people seeking to be loved. The family unit is in disarray due to all sorts of ungodly ideologies and philosophies regarding love and marriage. Very few people are standing for what is right because they don't want to hurt anyone's feelings! Children are being parented by standards set by the media.

If we were created in the Image of God, and made in His likeness, are we not supposed to act like Him? A mango tree can only produce mangoes. Do trees not produce fruit after their kind (Genesis 1:11-12)? An ambassador represents the values, standards, and opinions of their home country. Does not the Bible clearly state that we are ambassadors of Christ? Yet, how can we act like Jesus without ever opening up the Bible to find out how He acts and what He says about us?

LACK OF KNOWLEDGE IS DESTROYING THE FAMILY UNIT.

The lack of knowledge regarding the purpose of marriage is ruining the family unit. The real purpose of marriage has been attacked by an already defeated enemy! The fairy tale stories about marriage are what people expect in everyday life, and those unrealistic – therefore unfulfilled – expectations in marriage result in envy and self-seeking, which then leads to disorder and all forms of evil work (James 3:16).

What if every couple was told the truth before marriage? You can't get married with the expectation that your spouse will fulfill your desires and make you whole. Where did all these lies come from? They came from the father of all lies and the destroyer of marriage: the devil. Although your spouse may compliment you, they will never complete you. Only in Christ are we complete when we are united as one.

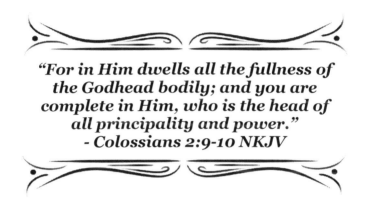

"For in Him dwells all the fullness of the Godhead bodily; and you are complete in Him, who is the head of all principality and power."
- Colossians 2:9-10 NKJV

Unity in Agreement

The purpose of marriage is unity. God's power is not only released in unity and in agreement, it is also multiplied! When a couple unites, they are able to conquer and subdue. Happiness, joy, peace, gentleness, contentment and love are provided by God. The Holy Spirit ministers all of these to our hearts. When we put our hope and trust in God, the Holy Spirit leads us into all truth about marriage.

Your spouse can't be a substitute for the Holy

Spirit, and your marriage can't replace the God-shaped vacuum in your life. Let the Holy Spirit be your source of happiness, joy, contentment, strength and peace.

God has given us His love through grace, but we have to access it by faith (Romans 5:2). We only have peace in marriage through Jesus Christ.

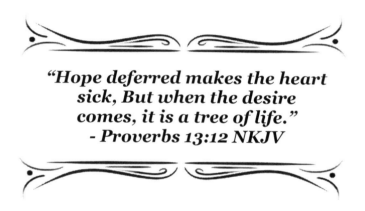

"Hope deferred makes the heart sick, But when the desire comes, it is a tree of life."
- Proverbs 13:12 NKJV

When this truth is spoken in love, then couples will begin to unite, and the family unit will be restored. Unity in marriage must be intentional.

God wants your marriage to succeed. He wants you to trust in His unfailing promises. He will put His desires in your heart. He wants to complete you, and He will when you make Him your source of hope, rather than your spouse. He wants you to agree with His promises for your life.

As a new bride, I quickly realized my husband was not my source, so I turned to The Tree of Life to sustain me. I knew that there had to be more in marriage than what I was experiencing, and I wanted it! Although running away sounded perfect, I determined that it was simply not an option – realistically I would only be running away from myself. However, I did not want to struggle with this on my own!

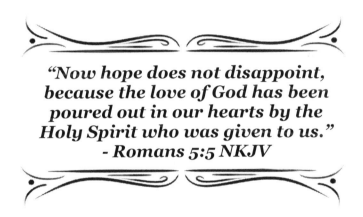

"Now hope does not disappoint, because the love of God has been poured out in our hearts by the Holy Spirit who was given to us."
- Romans 5:5 NKJV

The Titus 2 Ladies

Every married woman – and man -- should have a mentor. Regardless of how old you are when you first get married, you need an older woman to teach you how to love your husband, stand by you, and give you godly advice. The Holy Spirit will divinely connect your path with such people.

This woman does not need to be your birth

mother, or even a relative. However, she should be someone trustworthy with whom you can be vulnerable. (If your relationship with your mother is good and transparent, go ahead and use her! However, my advice is to keep motherly involvement in your marriage relationships to a minimum. I may be wrong, but I believe in healthy boundaries with parents – grow up by cutting the umbilical cord!)

Again, this lady must be honest, trust-worthy and one who will advise you without condemning your husband or taking sides. Keep in mind that she can condemn a **behavior** without condemning the

"That the older men be sober, reverent, temperate, sound in faith, in love, in patience; the older women likewise, that they be reverent in behavior, not slanderers, not given to much wine, teachers of good things - that they admonish the young women to love their husbands, to love their children, to be discreet, chaste, homemakers, good, obedient to their own husbands, that the word of God may not be blasphemed."
- Titus 2:2-5 NKJV

person. She should be a virtuous woman who will speak truth with love at all times. This person should be one who walks not in the counsel of the ungodly nor stands in the path of sinners. Her delight is to

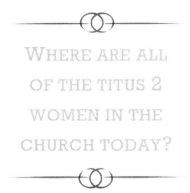

WHERE ARE ALL OF THE TITUS 2 WOMEN IN THE CHURCH TODAY?

stand on the promises of God with you for your marriage (Psalm 1:1-3). She drinks from the Fountain of Life that never runs dry, and from her fruit you will know she is a mature believer (Matthew 7:20).

I wondered, *Where are these Titus 2 women? Do they exist in the twenty-first century church? Where are the women and men that will speak the truth of proper and sound doctrine?* As I longed for answers, the Holy Spirit directed me to certain women.

I remember at the beginning of 2012, our pastor told us to ask God for a desire that would benefit the congregation. I took this assignment very seriously and prayed about it. Not long after, the Holy Spirit started reminding me of how I had desired strongly to have a mentor.

He reminded me of three women who had played a very important role in my marriage. I had learned very quickly not to share things about my marriage with just anyone. I gained wisdom from God that if someone wasn't praying with me, and for me, I would not tell them about my struggles.

These women had supported me by praying with me and listening to my struggles. They were open and vulnerable with me by sharing their own challenges; they were real women -- they were transparent. I realized that they were the women described in Titus 2. They were so important to me, I even named my second child after one of them.

I want to tell you about how God brought about divine appointments to ensure I received the Godly Titus 2 mentorship I so desperately needed, even though I was not aware that it was even addressed in scripture!

Our church administrator at that time was a very kind and loving lady. I admired Cyndy in many ways: her smiles and open heart were very welcoming, and she made sure the church functioned well. At the end of our monthly nursery leadership meeting, I requested to speak with her privately. As I explained what the Holy Spirit had been instructing me, she smiled and pulled out her Bible.

"Etonde," she said, "all of what you just told me is right in here. You are talking about the Titus 2 woman."

She read the passage to me, and I can't explain the joy in my heart at that very moment. God had spoken to me! He cares so much about young married women that He put scripture specifically to help guide them. One word from God can change your life! I can't tell you how many times I have read that passage.

Here is a question: do churches take the role of Titus 2 women seriously? Most ladies Bible study groups are not focused on mentorship, but this subject must be taken seriously because there are many women like my younger self in need of mentors. There are Christian women who are struggling in their marriage and have no one to whom they can open up. Even if they do open up to another woman, are the older women willing to be transparent?

Are they mature enough to use their past experiences as a teaching tool for younger couples? If not, it's possible that they have not healed from the past. Or, maybe they did not allow the power of the Holy Spirit to be manifested in that area. The truth is, if we don't deal with the horizontal aspects of our

ONE WORD FROM GOD CAN CHANGE YOUR LIFE!

lives – relationships with others: spouses, children, the brethren, siblings, relatives, etc. – they will affect our vertical relationships with God. For God to work through you, He must first do a work in you. It is impossible for you to give something that you don't have.

GOD LOOKS AT YOUR SPIRIT, NOT YOUR MISTAKES!

You can only minister out of the abundance that is inside of you. You reach out to others because your cup runs over due to your vertical relationship with your Heavenly Father. Doesn't God say, "Out of the abundance of the heart the mouth speaks" (Matthew 12:34)? To be effective, women need to step up into leadership and stop feeling condemned.

God looks at your spirit, not your mistakes. Don't let your heart condemn you; for God is greater than your heart (1 John 3:20). Your mess is a testimony that will set another couple free and save their marriage. Turn your mess into a ministry! Get your eyes off you, and let God heal you so that you can be His hands and feet. It is not enough to dress up, looking good, on Sunday mornings and be superficial in front of the young married couples at church.

It is not enough to tell a young bride that things will get better with time when, in reality, many marriages fail within the first few years. Be intentional about asking that young woman in your church how life is going for her. Take her out for lunch or invite her into your home.

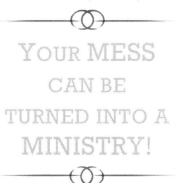

YOUR MESS CAN BE TURNED INTO A MINISTRY!

Be the Voice in Her Wilderness

She needs your wisdom. She is struggling inside, but so afraid to reach out for help due to the possibility of the voice of condemnation. All she sees on Sundays are women who seem to have everything figured out. They are nicely dressed, with perfect makeup, while she can barely find an outfit to wear, let alone makeup! She sees picture perfect families, in leadership positions, who are too busy to even say hello; she feels invisible. What she sees at Bible study are women who seem to know all the scriptures, and exactly what to say, while she can barely remember one verse.

Are you an older lady who is supposed to reach out to a younger bride? Are you too busy with life that you miss out on an opportunity to minister to her? Are you afraid that people will know how you also struggled? The mess in your past is a message that can encourage and heal another woman. Letting a young bride know your testimony can help her overcome her present situation.

LOOK FOR THE WOMEN IN YOUR CHURCH WHO MAY FEEL INVISIBLE.

So, have you noticed the new mom in your church lately? Have you taken time to know her name? Are you being busy as Martha and missing a ministry opportunity?

Start paying attention to the younger women in your church and community! Be intentional and sensitive to the lady sitting next to you, the one you meet in the bathroom, the young woman at bible study, the lady who always runs into church at the very last minute, the one in the parking lot, or the mother with a newborn or toddler that needs your loving and healing words.

Do you know such a lady? Have you seen her lately? Take time to ask her name! Be a voice of victory in her life. Are we not supposed to be God's mouthpiece? Be the voice of encouragement of one crying in her wilderness; there is hope when you stand on the promises of God.

I know someone needs this right now: God is working a new thing in your marriage this season and you shall know it. He is making a road for you in your wilderness and rivers in your desert. Your Heavenly Father knows your name for you are His. Fear not, for He is with you always. He will water your path and enrich you greatly. He will bless you abundantly in all you do. He has your name tattooed on the palms of His hands. Believe and receive!

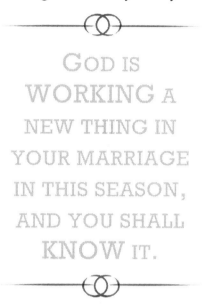

GOD IS WORKING A NEW THING IN YOUR MARRIAGE IN THIS SEASON, AND YOU SHALL KNOW IT.

Strength for Today

I had my first daughter in my final year of nursing school. This meant I had to work extra hard in everything due to very little sleep. God gives extra strength to mothers! My prayer for each day was, "God I need strength and wisdom just for today. Your

GOD'S
POWER IS
MADE
PERFECT
IN OUR
WEAKNESS!

grace is sufficient for me for your power is made known in my weakness."

One Sunday, during church service, my three-month-old daughter was a little loud, so I took her to the foyer. This way, I could still manage to listen to the sermon, while not disrupting the service. A lady walked toward me to say hello and asked how I was doing. How nice of her!

She invited me to Bible study and told me about a beneficial program for young mothers going on in our church. Mothers of Preschoolers – MOPS – was held twice a month on Tuesdays, but due to my school schedule it was impossible. However, I did tell her that I would try to make it to the Saturday Bible Study.

Despite my busy life as a wife, mother, and student, I managed to make it to the Bible study. It was a group of about six women. Although I had interacted with some of them in passing at church, they were mostly strangers to me. Our youth pastor's wife was leading the group. She was a lady I admired in many ways; she always had a welcoming smile and seemed to have everything put together.

We went through a Beth Moore Study, and although I don't remember what the topic was, I remember it was good! I barely finished my readings before the class, but at least I showed up and listened. One day, I poured out my heart to the women in this group. I could not stop crying while sharing my struggles at home. I had finally found a safe ground where I could just talk and cry.

Meet Kay

Allow me to introduce my first Titus 2 mentor, Kay. Kay is the lady who was sensitive to her environment and took the bold step to invite me to Bible study and told me about MOPS. She was inten-

COMPASSION CARES FOR A STRUGGLING BRIDE AND NEW MOTHER.

tional about reaching out to a young mother with a three-month-old crying child sitting out of service. She reached out in love. Compassion cares for a struggling bride and new mother. There are many women in your own church waiting for you to reach out and invite them to an activity.

"Let the redeemed of The Lord say so, Whom He has re-deemed from the hands of the enemy."
- Psalm 107:2 NKJV

One Saturday, during Bible study, Kay asked me to pray about finding a lady who I could talk to. Little did she know that God had already placed **her** in my heart, but I just did not know how to start the conversation. So, because of my hesitation, the Holy Spirit simply prompted her to ask me! I quickly walked through the door He had opened for me and told her she was that lady!

She took a deep breath and responded with, "Oh, wow!"

I think she was surprised when I reacted so quickly to her suggestion that I pray for a mentor! But, why would I pray about something when I already knew the answer?

Kay was a godsend in my life – she was truly God sent! She invited me for lunch at Panera Bread, where we first formed a friendship. She not only listened to me, but she also opened up to me about her own life. She encouraged me in being a godly wife to my husband.

One significant lesson Kay taught me was the power of the Holy Spirit. At that stage, I had totally checked out emotionally from my husband and was actually ready to check out completely. As we continued to meet at Panera Bread for our mentor dates, I opened up to her about every struggle in my life.

She asked me if I wanted her husband to have a man speak with my husband. Now, it is always preferable for a man to talk to another man – specifically, I mean a **godly** man speaking truth into another man's life. However, I was not sure how my husband would take this. I was afraid he would take it as though I had been talking badly about him behind his back! This was the perfect opportunity for her to begin to teach me about the Holy Spirit.

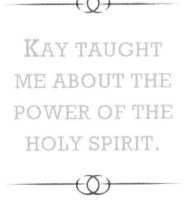

KAY TAUGHT ME ABOUT THE POWER OF THE HOLY SPIRIT.

While meditating on this, Kay told me she believed in the power of the Holy Spirit.

"Why don't we pray for the Holy Spirit to minister to your husband before we set up a meeting with my husband?" she suggested.

This sounded to me like a perfect idea. Before we left that date, she encouraged me to, "let go and let God!"

You Are Not the Holy Spirit

Are you in need of another man to talk to your husband? Are you going around telling all your marital troubles to everyone? How about you just let go and trust the Holy Spirit to do the work for you? You will never be a good Holy Spirit. Only the Holy Spirit can change the hearts of men – not you.

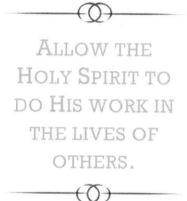

ALLOW THE HOLY SPIRIT TO DO HIS WORK IN THE LIVES OF OTHERS.

Due to my past encounters with God, I knew that He speaks to us. This is a huge topic for another book, but I mention that because it's funny how when we pray for our husbands, the Holy Spirit starts speaking to us about ourselves first! I wanted a change in my home, but He had to start with me.

I had to "harden not my heart" and enter into God's rest (Hebrews 3:15 & 4:1). My heart had been hardened with things from my past that had built walls in me. There were thorns and bushes that needed to be pulled out – things that I did not know would affect my marriage relation-ship.

Those things brought unnecessary conflicts in our commu-nication. Your spouse can mean good, but past hurts can turn things around in an instant.

> PAST HURTS CAN CAUSE INSTANT RESPONSES THAT CAN RESULT IN UNNECESSARY CONFLICTS.

At one point, there was no communication be-tween my husband and I at all, except in matters con-cerning our daughter. Yes, we were living in the same house and sleeping on the same bed. The baby oc-cupied the in between space that separated the two of us. I still made him warm meals after work. Yet, the only life in our home was our happy baby trying to get our attention.

At that time in our relationship, I remember very well driving to Walmart one day when compassion came upon my heart. I began to miss my husband!

So, after parking the car, my spirit prompted me

to send him a text message. My flesh did not want to do this, but I submitted to my spirit and sent out the message, anyway.

It was such a simple message, "Just want to let you know I'm thinking about you!"

IT CAN BE HARD TO ACT IN KINDNESS TO SOMEONE, ESPECIALLY IF YOU FEEL THEY ARE UNDESERVING.

Are you at this place in your marriage? I know it hurts! I've been there before, and I relate to your struggles. It can be very hard to act in kindness and compassion to someone, especially when you feel that they do not deserve it.

Yet, this text message was the ice breaker that led to us conceiving our second daughter. As I reached out to my husband, in obedience to the leading of the Holy Spirit, it softened his heart toward me. This one simple act of obedience, in humility, is what ultimately led to our reconciliation!

What the Holy Spirit can do, no man can. Because we had allowed the Holy Spirit minister to our hearts, He also blessed us with another baby! I went from planning an escape, to the thought of having another baby, all because I submitted to the voice of compassion in the midst of my wilderness.

My next meeting with Kay at Panera Bread was full of laughter. She asked me how things were going, and I´told her was pregnant! She asked me how things were going at home. I shared with her that the Holy Spirit had done some heart work on me! My heart had softened, became rested and was at peace with God.

I also told Kay that I had looked up the meaning of her name and would name my daughter after her. Kay means "Rejoice," and the Lord surely brought laughter into our home!

Meet Jacky

Now, I also want to tell you about Jacky, another Titus 2 lady! Where do I even start to explain how thankful I am to Jacky and her family? She was the one who made me realize that my marriage was at war, but that my husband was not the enemy!

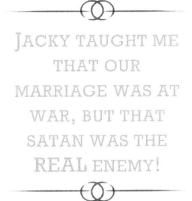

JACKY TAUGHT ME THAT OUR MARRIAGE WAS AT WAR, BUT THAT SATAN WAS THE REAL ENEMY!

Jacky and her husband were leaders

of our small group at the church we attended. She would listen to me talk and remind me that the enemy was the problem. She encouraged me to always stand **with** my husband against the enemy. This greatly changed my thinking on many things, but it wasn't until many years later that I fully understood what she meant.

Strife at home is the breeding ground for attacks against the family. The enemy takes advantage of strife and envy. He will kill, steal, and destroy your home. Once we got this revelation, we made the effort to intentionally live in peace together, with the help of the Holy Spirit. Forgiving each other is key in getting rid of strife at home.

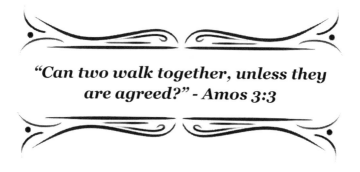

"Can two walk together, unless they are agreed?" - Amos 3:3

Team work is very important. When we look at the Trinity we see teamwork. The Father plans, the Son performs, and the Holy Spirit empowers. If God works as a team, shouldn't we do the same? Couples will conquer and subdue giants if they stand in agreement. If one can put a thousand to flight, then two will put ten thousand to flight (Deuteronomy 32:30). Agreeing as a couple is the only way you will reign in your relationship. Nothing will be able to come against you!

"Wives, submit to your own husbands, as is fitting in the Lord."
- Colossians 3:18 NKJV

Am I saying there will not be times you disagree? No! Disagreement will come, but the wife will have to submit, and agree to get rid of strife. Even Jesus had to submit to the Father to go to the cross for our sake (Matthew 26:39). We have to do likewise by exalting God's Word as the final say in any disagreement.

The enemy will do everything possible to bring division and confusion into your marriage, especially if you are not walking in agreement. Many couples today are simply sharing a roof. They can't agree on anything; from how to raise the children to buying groceries – you name it. Their bank accounts are separate; their family has no common purpose.

Since there is no unity, they have no vision for their family! Their focus is split between individual projects and pursuits. It is impossible for a troop to defeat an enemy if they are not united in their mission.

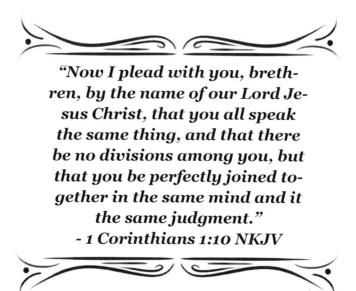

"Now I plead with you, brethren, by the name of our Lord Jesus Christ, that you all speak the same thing, and that there be no divisions among you, but that you be perfectly joined together in the same mind and it the same judgment."
- 1 Corinthians 1:10 NKJV

There must be a commander that gives directions. Any soldier who does not follow the plan of action exposes the entire army to their enemy. Who is your captain? Who pilots your plane?

Look at this: Father God devised the plan to redeem man, Jesus had to agree with Him and perform the plan, and the Holy Spirit agreed and empowered

Jesus to carry it out. Even when Jesus asked the Father to take the cup away from Him, if possible, the Holy Spirit was right there to give Jesus the strength to finish the will of the Father. All three of them accomplished the redemption of man.

Think about what you can, and will, accomplish as a couple united in Christ. Couples who can't agree expose their families to the enemy. Not agreeing is giving the bullet to the enemy to shoot right at you. Your kids

COUPLES WHO CAN'T AGREE EXPOSE THEIR FAMILIES TO THE ENEMY.

will manipulate you if you are not united in word. You have to speak the same language all the time. Purpose in your hearts to be a couple of integrity. Your kids need to know that what Dad says, Mom will approve and agree with, and vice versa.

If you can't agree with your spouse, whom you can see, how then will you agree with your Heavenly Father whom you can't see? Not agreeing with your spouse is agreeing with the enemy who seeks to destroy you. I'm not talking about bad behavior or the character of a spouse. I'm talking about unity in decision making and pursuing vision. You have to be going in the same direction.

You see, God has given you His Word. All you need to do is agree with Him. The Word became flesh and has made His dwelling within us. Are you going to let Him be the Captain of your marriage? Will you let him be your pilot?

The copilot only does what the pilot tells him; the copilot submits to the leadership of the pilot. They must agree with each other to reach their destination. All that the Father has belongs to the Son. In turn, He has extended to you all that He has so that your marriage can succeed. Will you agree with Him and reach out and receive? His hand is already extended, waiting for you to reach out to Him.

AGREE WITH YOUR SPOUSE, AND WITH YOUR HEAVENLY FATHER.

AGREE WITH GOD, SUBMIT TO HIS LEADERSHIP, AND ALLOW HIM TO TAKE YOU TO YOUR DESTINATION.

This is why Jesus came: so that we could agree and walk together to achieve His greater purpose. His power is released when we walk together in unity. When you agree with His Son, you are cooperating with Him. The more we agree with His Word, the more we are being conformed into His image (Romans 8:29).

Jesus is the Living Word! God has given us His written Word. The written Word becomes the Living Word in your life when you agree with Him. His power is made manifest when you simply agree with what He says in His Word.

What are you believing for today concerning your marriage? Agree with the Living Word and speak it over your life. Speak only what God speaks and don't speak your problem. We were created to live only by the words that proceed from the mouth of the Father. Magnify the Living Word. By doing so, you are calling those things that do not exist in the physical realm as if they do (Romans 4:17).

Are you agreeing with God who can't change His Word? See every impossibility in your life as possible when you agree with the Living Word. God has exalted His Word above His Name. He has exalted Jesus above His Name. Do you agree

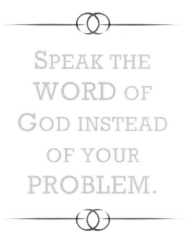

SPEAK THE WORD OF GOD INSTEAD OF YOUR PROBLEM.

with Jesus? Humility is agreeing with God. Disagreeing with your spouse and the Living Word is rebelling against God's promises for you.

Chapter Five

Strife Will Destroy Your Marriage

Living in strife is demonic. This is something many couples do not think about, and we were one of those. Strife and envy is the root of every evil work. Self-seeking is a very dangerous thing and only leads to strife. When you understand that quarrels and contentious behaviors open the door for the enemy into your home, you will strive to get rid of it.

Let me ask you a question: who brings about confusion? God is not the author of confusion, but the God of peace. God is an orderly God. Do I need to tell you anymore who causes confusion and strife in your home? The enemy does! He is the father of lies and disorder (John 8:44).

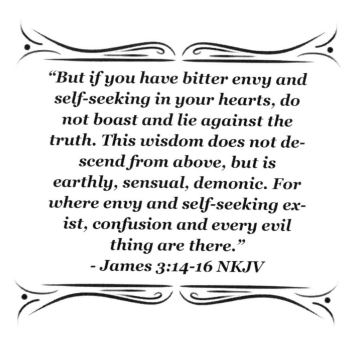

"But if you have bitter envy and self-seeking in your hearts, do not boast and lie against the truth. This wisdom does not descend from above, but is earthly, sensual, demonic. For where envy and self-seeking exist, confusion and every evil thing are there."
- James 3:14-16 NKJV

So, whenever you find yourself throwing curse words around, and quarreling with your spouse, know that you are giving free access to the enemy into your home. You are cooperating with the enemy to destroy it. A person who sows discord – as in loves to knock heads together and manipulate others – is an agent straight from hell. The Bible describes manipulation as the sin of witchcraft. Calamity will overtake you. I don't know about you, but I know people like this! It is very important that couples should be able to recognize that maintaining peace in their home is a priority.

Have you ever entered into a home and sensed the tension in the atmosphere? Many couples don't realize that strife changes the environment. Evil spirits take over your home. You find your kids always sick and you wonder why. A crushed spirit dries up bones! The enemy will take advantage and ruin your family.

But how do I get rid of strife and envy with my spouse? Well, forgive! Un-forgiveness breeds strife. Let go!

Divorce this evil spirit that is manipulating you. Your spouse is not the enemy! Separate yourselves from the spirit of strife. It is simple: be transparent with each other and learn to listen first be-

EVERY WORD YOU SPEAK IS A SEED YOU ARE PLANTING.

fore you make any decisions. Do not make assumptions and come to your own conclusions. Think before you speak. Every word you speak is a seed you are planting: you will reap the harvest! Work together, as a couple, not against each other. Unity in decision making is key to a successful home.

Shut up!

Shut up! Zip your lips! Know the right time to say the right thing. Saying the right thing during a quarrel only escalates things. Two wrongs don't make a right. What good does it do you to repay evil for evil? Does God not tell us to repay evil with good? One important lesson the Holy Spirit taught me was to learn to shut up.

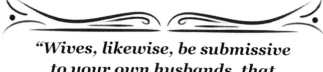

"Wives, likewise, be submissive to your own husbands, that even if some do not obey the word, they, without a word, may be won by the conduct of their wives, when they observe your chaste conduct accompanied by fear."
- 1 Peter 3:1-2 NKJV

The ability to submit without a word is letting the Holy Spirit take charge. Being **meek** does not mean you are **weak**. Being meek is yielding to the Holy Spirit to work in you and through you. A meek spirit submits first to God because they trust God to perform that which He promised.

HUMILITY IS NOT WEAKNESS, IT IS LEADERSHIP.

Say you are sorry for peace's sake! Humility is leadership, it does not mean you are weak. Let the Holy Spirit lead your decisions and help you discern and recognize this spirit. Think about the impact of your words before you say them. Let your words be encouraging and not discouraging.

Strife is an evil spirit that has been defeated on the cross. You give it power when you fail to recognize its manipulative skills. Jesus came to disarm principalities and powers; He made a public spectacle of them, triumphing over them all (Colossians 2:15).

I want you to know that you have power over the enemy because you are more than conqueror in Christ. You execute judgement over the enemy when you get rid of strife in your home by speaking words of peace and edification. Therefore, you give the enemy no access to ruin your family. Always stand with God's Word: speak the truth. When you speak the truth, you are speaking Jesus and the enemy must bow at the mention of the name Jesus (Romans 8:37, Philippians 2:10).

Identify Weeds

Another very important way to get rid of strife in our homes is to identify "weeds and thorns". It's very easy for weeds to ruin your lawn if you don't get rid of them in time. Weeds can become thorns that will choke the life out of you. What am I saying? Everyone has weeds that will pop up in their marriages. Most likely they are from past hurts, or from the environment – culture to which your families have been exposed. If not dealt with, they can become walls and layers of strongholds.

UNTENDED WEEDS CAN RUIN YOUR LAWN!

It is easy to admire your neighbor's lawn while your lawn looks very bad. What you don't realize is that your neighbor is intentional about tending his lawn. He plans ahead as the seasons change and fertilizes it multiple times in the spring. He identifies the weeds and uses weed killer to get rid of bad grass. He takes time to mow the lawn twice a week in the summer. At the beginning of autumn, he winterizes the lawn to get it ready for winter. After winter, he again watches the weather as it gets warmer to make sure he starts on time with his lawn care. All you see is the result of his labor: a perfect summer lawn!

While he was cultivating his lawn, you were busy with the cares of life and paid no attention to your own. Yet, you wonder why your lawn is in it's horrible state. You see, couples who are intentional about their marriages will notice weeds when they pop up. They intentionally and quickly pull them up before they can do any damage.

They notice as the seasons of life change and prepare for the next season. They don't wait for weeds – crisis and cares of this life – to pop up before they seek help. They plan ahead and look for remedies for killing weeds. They understand that "one ounce of prevention is better than one pound of cure!"

SUCCESSFUL COUPLES WILL QUICKLY PULL WEEDS BEFORE THEY CAUSE DAMAGE.

They do maintenance therapy.

What steps are you taking to work on your marriage? Are you letting weeds grow like a dandelion in your yard? Have past hurts built walls in your heart which are preventing you from receiving and growing? Are you stuck because of weeds in your life?

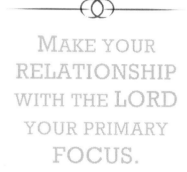

MAKE YOUR RELATIONSHIP WITH THE LORD YOUR PRIMARY FOCUS.

I have good news for you. There is hope in Jesus Christ. This is why He came: to help you care for your marriage and to identify weeds holding you captive.

First you have to work on your marriage with Him. Your first marriage is that with the Prince of Peace, and second that with your spouse. He is the gardener! Let him teach you how to identify weeds in your life from past hurts. You will need to spend some time with Him. It does not take a day to learn all the lessons from the Gardener. It is year-round training – a life long journey. He wants your lawn to look even better than your neighbor's.

Stop admiring your neighbor's lawn and get to work on your own! It takes time and patience to have a good marriage. Be a good gardener by abiding with the Gardener. He wants to prune you, so that you may bear much fruit.

"I am the vine, you are the branches. He who abides in Me, and I in him, bears much fruit; for without Me you can do nothing."
– John 15:5 NKJV

www.victorynowmin.org

Chapter Six

Behind the Scenes: Miscarriage

When Cinderella and Prince Charming start off in life, the last thing they are thinking of is losing a baby. No one ever imagines this when they get married, and the same was true for me. The happily-ever-after hoax does not prepare a couple for when tragedy becomes a reality. That was my experience on three separate occasions. Didn't God say there shall be no miscarriage in the land?

I realize that many couples are dealing with issues that, due to their culture, are taboo to talk about.

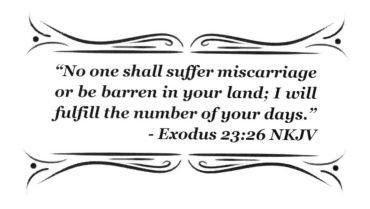

"No one shall suffer miscarriage or be barren in your land; I will fulfill the number of your days."
- Exodus 23:26 NKJV

Yet, how will they heal from this hurt if no one talks about it? Hearts are broken and need healing! It is a thorn stabbing many hearts in marriages where the outside picture never really portrays the entire behind-the-scenes story. It can surely paint an eye-catching facade. However, what we see physically may be deceiving and hides both the joy and pain that is going on inside.

WHAT WE SEE PHYSICALLY CAN HIDE BOTH JOY AND PAIN.

Looks can be very deceiving and never should one draw conclusions about the inside by what is seen on the outside. Wait until people open their mouths honestly, then you will know the condition of their hearts. Remember, out of the heart flow the issues of life.

When we look at Instagram, or Facebook, today, we see beautiful pictures of the current outside states of people. What most people don't think about is what is really happening on the inside. What is going on behind the scenes of the lives of the people taking these pictures?

Your inside story is different and unique to you yet can bring healing to another. Inside stories are meant to be told. This is my story.

> **YOUR INSIDE STORY IS UNIQUE, YET CAN BRING HEALING TO ANOTHER.**

I will continuously recite my composition concerning my Creator. My heart overflows with a good theme (Psalm 45:1). I have chosen to magnify the Cross and not my loss. When I walk into any room with my girls, what you don't see are three other children who are missing on this side of Heaven. What most women don't know, or sometimes even think about, before they get married are the challenges in the process of child bearing.

Unexpected loss in this process can break relationships. I've always wanted a big family. I had written on my goal board, before I met my husband, that I wanted eight kids. He was shocked the first time he visited my apartment. Who in this day and age wants eight kids, right?

My plan was clear, and he knew it; I was not changing my mind about this. Believe it or not, I was an answer to his prayers. He always prayed for a woman willing to have more babies than the current cultural norm of two to three. The philosophy was "the more the better!" Anyway, we started out with the big family idea, and we are not giving up anytime soon!

Our first pregnancy happened very quickly and talk about excitement and emotions! My body reacted strangely: I exploded overnight, and my figure literally became disfigured from what was normal.

DURING MY FIRST VISIT TO THE HOSPITAL, I WAS ASKED IF I WAS GOING TO KEEP MY BABY!

What was even more scary was when I walked into the hospital for the first time and was asked whether I wanted to keep, or do away with, the baby. **I left that place really angry!**

"I see you are pregnant. What do you plan on doing – will you keep the baby?"

Babies are meant to be born, not killed. Don't ask me that! Not only had my body changed, a medical professional was now **speaking death** over my baby.

About twelve weeks later, we had a spontaneous abortion. My body aborted our first baby! Talk about devastation. I was asking all kinds of questions. A bad scene in a movie was my realty.

BABIES ARE MEANT TO BE BORN, NOT KILLED.

What in the world just happened?

About a year later, we conceived for the second time. She is now who everyone sees as my first daughter; Njuamboh is my "rainbow baby," as they call it. She is such a smart thinker, and dreamer, and is my second blessing from God. The enemy stole the life of my first baby.

Twenty-two months later came our third baby, Ngeniform. She is who everyone else knows to be our second daughter. This little girl lights up the room and brings a lot of laughter to our home!

My daughters don't yet know that they had an older sibling. I will tell them when the time is right.

After carrying two babies to full-term, everything

looked normal and fine. Even though I sometimes imagined what this baby would have looked and acted like, the pain and grief of losing my first child was gone.

Yet, in 2015, we lost another baby through a miscarriage. I shared this experience with my friends hoping to pass a message: you don't wish this on anyone.

It was at this point when I found the truth of who God really is. All my life, until this time, I did not understand the true nature of God. Religion taught me that God gives and takes away, but why would He kill my babies to teach me something? **Why would a loving God kill your child?** God cannot be tempted by evil (James 1:13).

RELIGION SAYS THAT GOD GIVES AND TAKES AWAY, BUT WHY WOULD A LOVING GOD KILL MY CHILD?

When I lost my first baby, I was told several reasons: the stronger babies survive; God took the baby back because He needed an angel; we are going through this because I did something wrong; maybe there was a deformity; God is teaching me a lesson, and so on.

After the second loss, I needed answers. I wanted to know exactly what went wrong. Why did her heart stop beating at twelve weeks? If God is the giver of life, then He should have an answer. So, I went directly to Him with all my questions.

GOD HAS A PLAN AND PURPOSE FOR EVERY SINGLE CHILD!

What I found was a Father full of righteousness, peace and joy. This is what He told me:

"My daughter, I don't make mistakes when I form babies; neither do I kill babies before they are born. I don't teach you a lesson by inflicting pain on you. Babies are not angels, so I don't need baby angels by killing babies. Every gift I bless my children with is perfect. I have a plan and a purpose for every child born. My desire is for them to live to a full lifespan.

WE LIVE IN A WORLD THAT HAS BEEN CHANGED BY SIN.

The world is not what it used to be at creation: you live in a fallen world. Sin changed the world. There is an enemy whose desire is to kill, steal and destroy

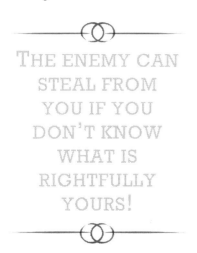

THE ENEMY CAN STEAL FROM YOU IF YOU DON'T KNOW WHAT IS RIGHTFULLY YOURS!

anything good that I have given you. You cooperate with him by what you believe and speak. He takes advantage of your lack of knowledge of My Truth. He steals from you because you don't know what is rightfully yours.

No sickness can survive in my presence. Death was nailed to the cross; I AM life-giving. When you know the Truth, you will be set free and have fullness of joy. You have to take authority over your problems. The Kingdom of God suffers violence and the violent must take it by force. You are being violated by the enemy and not by Me. I AM Love!"

Wait a minute, all that I had been told were lies! God is not a killer of babies – a baby murderer as He is regarded by many. He **gives life**; He is love, joy, and peace, which can only be found in Him. He is the Truth we must find to help us navigate through life. He loves our babies even more than we do. He has given us a manual to teach us how to bring them up.

All we need is to open The Book and fall in love with the Creator God. Yet, even when we do, the enemy will still send giants our way to distract us.

In the fall of 2016, we got pregnant again with our fifth child. Nine weeks later, yet again, the enemy cut this life short. Now, this was a big distraction, but our eyes were fixed on the cross. We only understand in part now, but we know without a doubt that all three of our babies are alive with Christ. They will welcome us on the other side of Heaven when we are satisfied with life on Earth at an old age.

Each day I wonder what their personalities would have been, how funny they would have been, and the interesting things they would have done. However, I know for sure they are alive and not dead; they will never be forgotten because I carried them. My body changed because of them, I think differently because of them, and I dream of them. God wrote their names in my heart.

GOD LOVES OUR BABIES EVEN MORE THAN WE DO.

To those who are reading this: I don't know what your behind-the-scene story is. You may be angry with God or depressed over the loss of a child. You may be wondering why bad things are happening to you, or why other ladies seem more blessed than you are. Life may seem unfair and cruel in your eyes.

STOP BLAMING GOD AND START PRAISING!

But, I have good news for you. Lift up your eyes, shake off the dust from the past, and focus on the cross instead of the loss. Always magnify Jesus, despite your current situation. God will do a new thing in your life, it shall spring forth and you shall know it (Isaiah 43:19). You will be reunited with your babies on the other side of heaven. Stop blaming God and start praising Him.

To the unmarried young lady, with the perfect body: there will be changes and challenges along the way. Do not be alarmed by them. In this world you will have troubles, but take heart for Jesus overcame, which makes you an overcomer (John 16:33, 1 John 5:4-5). Start speaking life over your body today.

Do not accept all that the world throws at you. God's Word should always have the final say and become your truth. Let challenges build you up rather than break you. Take care of that temple you see in the mirror, yet focus more on renewing your mind with the truth of God's Word. Knowing the truth makes life more joyful, despite the giants along the way. Your giants must bow

START SPEAKING LIFE OVER YOUR BODY TODAY!

at the mention of the Name Jesus. Jesus has already defeated every giant that will ever show up in your life.

To the married couple trying to have a baby after a loss: be encouraged and never stop praising your Creator. He gives life to dead bodies and desires for you to conceive and carry your baby to term. If He did it for Sarah at ninety years old, He will do it for you. He delights when you are at peace and joyful with your gift. Don't give up on trying.

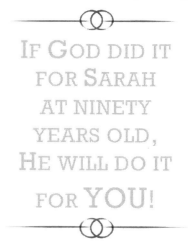

IF GOD DID IT FOR SARAH AT NINETY YEARS OLD, HE WILL DO IT FOR YOU!

Continue to speak life-giving words over your body each day. Ask God to give you a vision of your family, with children playing around you. Stand on His promises by speaking them out loud daily so your own ears can hear them. Faith comes by hearing and hearing by the Word of God (Romans 10:17).

FAITH SPEAKS

His Word is Life. Faith speaks! There is no behind-the-scene giant Jesus didn't nail to the cross. I speak healing over your entire body today, in Jesus' Name! To all couples wanting to conceive, more children are coming your way. Barren wombs: be open in Jesus' Name. I speak healthy and strong sperm in your husbands, in Jesus' Name. All ovarian diseases are dead, in Jesus' Name. Healthy babies shall be born in your family this season. Let God be true, and every bad word spoken over you be destroyed. By the stripes of Jesus, you are healed. Do you receive this? If so, speak your agreement with His Word with the Amen!

"I am strong because Jesus is my strength and confidence. I have favor with God and favor with man! I am a partaker of His Royal Kingdom. I walk in victory not as a victim."

Not every portrait tells the entire story. My story is unique to me. Your behind-the-scene story is meant to be told.

¹⁶ Therefore it is of faith that it might be according to grace, so that the promise might be sure to all the seed, not only to those who are of the law, but also to those who are of the faith of Abraham, who is the father of us all ¹⁷ (as it is written, "I have made you a father of many nations") in the presence of Him whom he believed—God, who gives life to the dead and calls those things which do not exist as though they did; ¹⁸ who, contrary to hope, in hope believed, so that he became the father of many nations, according to what was spoken, "So shall your descendants be." ¹⁹ And not being weak in faith, he did not consider his own body, already dead (since he was about a hundred years old), and the deadness of Sarah's womb. ²⁰ He did not waver at the promise of God through unbelief, but was strengthened in faith, giving glory to God, ²¹ and being fully convinced that what He had promised He was also able to perform. ²² And therefore "it was accounted to him for righteousness." ²³ Now it was not written for his sake alone that it was imputed to him, ²⁴ but also for us. It shall be imputed to us who believe in Him who raised up Jesus our Lord from the dead, ²⁵ who was delivered up because of our offenses, and was raised because of our justification."
- Romans 4:16-25 NKJV

Chapter Seven

Love is a Seed

One of the most precious possessions I have from my dad is a letter he wrote to me in August 20th, 2010. This is when I had come to the end of myself and had mentally checked out of my marriage. I told my dad I could not take it any longer. I was ready to leave that to which I had cleaved. My happily ever after literally was about to end. It sure was a hoax!

I do want to make it clear that there was no physical abuse. We just could not communicate with each other without a quarrel. There was no trust, due to thorns from our past that had not been healed; we had lot of scars that needed healing. What my dad told me brought light to my darkness. He was a voice in my wilderness.

I did not understand half of what he wrote back then. Yet, one thing was certain, this letter was not just for me. I knew that I would someday share this letter with many hurting couples. My prayer is that it will bring healing and restoration to your marriage just as it did for mine.

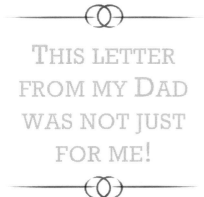

THIS LETTER FROM MY DAD WAS NOT JUST FOR ME!

In the latter years of my dad's life he was a marriage counselor. He wrote this letter sitting at his desk as a mayor of the Bamenda II counsel, where he lived in Cameroon, West Africa. One of his duties as a mayor was to counsel and marry couples in the civil court.

This letter is what couples received from him during their counseling sessions. The time came for him to do the same for his beautiful daughter, whose walls were crumbling down. He had so much wisdom because of his relationship with God. I consider this letter a gift from a loving father to his daughter.

"My Dear Daughter,

I would like to share with you some views that concern not only you but all of us. The first is that once a boy or girl comes of age, the natural urge is for them to look for their life partner. Some succeed; some fail. You cannot blame any person who fails to find a partner.

For those who succeed to find partners, they have a herculean task of discovering themselves. You see, two individuals who were raised under different circumstances are coming together to live out their lives. For the rest of their lives, they have to face life's challenges together, working hand in hand to raise their own children, and family, and to build up their lives.

COUPLES MUST FACE LIFE'S CHALLENGES TOGETHER.

At the onset, these two persons do not know themselves. They have to discover their individual characters over the years. Quite often, the hide-and-seek game goes on for years. This period may be referred to as their period of hibernation. At this time, many things may go wrong. It depends on how each other plays the game.

You see, as I just said, my dear daughter, two can never be the same. They think and act differently. This, being in the nature of things, they must learn to accept each other while over-looking the little una-voidable inadequacies of each other. It has to be so, because we all have our various shortcomings and different idiosyncrasies.

THEY MUST LEARN TO ACCEPT EACH OTHER.

One point stands out clearly in marriage: the man is head of the family and leads the way through the course of the union. The woman must accept her ordained role of a helper. She is under the man, but not necessarily under his foot to be trampled upon. She must be humble at all times, and never raise her voice above that of the man. Under all circumstances her disposition must remain calm, her voice soft but firm.

She must be a Calponia (Caesar's wife) who was above suspicion.

It should be noted that no man likes to be given orders, and, do not be mistaken, men like to be petted just like women do. Just like women like to feel wanted, men feel exactly the same way. A man feels on top of the world when he re-

turns home to the embracing arms of a loving, caring, comforting wife; to a warm home full of laughter and sunshine. He feels like a king when the wife he loves reminds him of her constant love and commitment – that she adores him. Yes! That he is always the man of her dreams, her king. It goes without saying too much that she is un-questionably the woman of his dreams and his queen. This whole thing is reciprocal. Bang, it is a give and take game.

My dear daughter, love is like a seed that you plant in the ground. You prepare the ground and make it ready to receive the seed. Once it is  *planted, there must be enough moisture to enable the seed to sprout. When the growing process commences, you continue to nurse it and guard the growing plant against predators. You do this until the plant matures and, even then, you do not lose your guard, because predators can still set in at any time. This nursing/protecting process in a marriage setting is continuous because mar-riage is a living thing. Both parties must get en-gaged in this nursing and protecting game.*

I hope that what I am saying makes some

sense to you. I want you to pay greater attention to what I say because it is for your good.

Finally, you must understand that marriage is not a bed of roses. You will surely meet with problems along the way as you go. Your strength will be measured by your ability to solve these problems without breaking bones. One of the surest way to solve these, or some, problems is your ability to appreciate where you go wrong and make amends rapidly. Make apologies and create a harmonious environment in your home.

Never, never create a situation of doubt as you go along. If one occurs, as it must at times, make sure that you clear it before the sun sets.

We love you very much daughter and pray that God should guide you as you strive to build your own home and raise your own children (our grandchildren).

We, also, love and respect your dear husband, whom we see as a perfect gentleman. He should be your icon.

Your Father,

Francis Achiri Ade"

I cannot tell you how many times I've read this letter! I actually did so at his funeral, in August 2015. It was the first time it was read publicly. This letter from my father is very deep, as you can see. Three months after he passed away, the Holy Spirit revealed to me what he was saying in a portion of his letter: love is a seed. This section contains a lot of wisdom on marriage, so I would like to highlight it again:

"My dear daughter, love is like a seed that you plant in the ground. You prepare the ground and make it ready to receive the seed. Once it is planted there must be enough moisture to enable the seed to sprout. When the growing process commences, you continue to nurse it and guard the growing plant against predators. You do this until the plant matures and even then, you do not loose guard because predators can still set in at any time. This nursing/protecting process in a marriage setting is continuous because marriage is a living thing. Both parties must get engaged in this nursing and protecting game."

Back then, I really did not understand this content, the way I do now. I listened to him and stayed with my husband, a decision I'm very thankful I made.

Listen to what he said, "Love is like a seed."

Do you see the parable of the sower in this letter? This is a kingdom principle that also applies in marriage (Mark 4). I get so much from this now!! God is Love. The Word of God is love. The Word of God is a seed that we must plant in our hearts. Love – the Word – is a seed we must plant in our marriages. We must plant the Word of God in our marriage relationships.

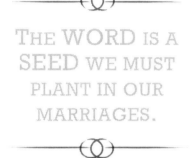

THE WORD IS A SEED WE MUST PLANT IN OUR MARRIAGES.

Agape love is what we are talking about here. Agape love came into the world when Jesus was born. God planted love into the world when He sent Jesus. We must continue in the Word to sustain our

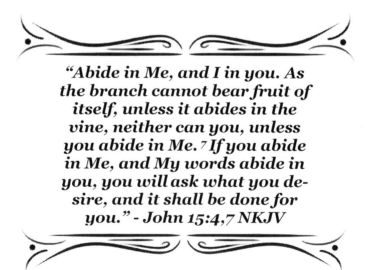

"Abide in Me, and I in you. As the branch cannot bear fruit of itself, unless it abides in the vine, neither can you, unless you abide in Me. 7 If you abide in Me, and My words abide in you, you will ask what you desire, and it shall be done for you." - John 15:4,7 NKJV

marriages. The Word – Jesus – is the sustaining power of marriage. Jesus is the Word, Jesus is the Seed.

Continuing in the Word is key in walking in victory; by so doing you are being a disciple of Jesus. There is no other way out of difficult situations than for us to abide in the Word. Abiding in the Word is abiding in Love.

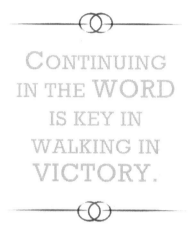

CONTINUING IN THE WORD IS KEY IN WALKING IN VICTORY.

We must prepare and continue to water our hearts for it to mature. We have to refill our spiritual tank with the Word of God.

"And we have known and be-lieved the love that God has for us. God is love, and he who abides in love abides in God, and God in him."
- I John 4:16 NKJV

You must never lose guard of this seed of love; if you do, predators will come and kill it. Predators are bad weeds in the parable of the sower and include all the attacks the enemy throws at our marriages. If we plant love – the Word of God – in our hearts and marriages, then we will be able to stand against the (already defeated) schemes of the enemy. We can't lose guard of love – again, the Word of God – because it is a living thing.

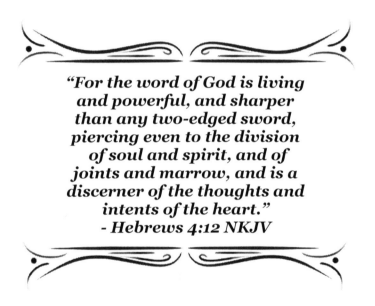

"For the word of God is living and powerful, and sharper than any two-edged sword, piercing even to the division of soul and spirit, and of joints and marrow, and is a discerner of the thoughts and intents of the heart."
- Hebrews 4:12 NKJV

I could go on and on in explaining the revelation hidden in my dad's words to me, but all I can say here is that he was a gift from God to me. I will be forever thankful to God for his life. He showed me what true love is: love was at the very beginning of the world.

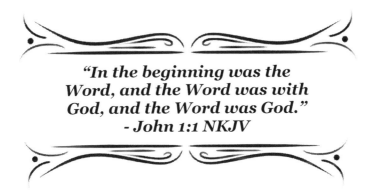

*"In the beginning was the
Word, and the Word was with
God, and the Word was God."
- John 1:1 NKJV*

This is how I read this passage:

"In the beginning was Love/Jesus,

and Love/Jesus was with God,

and Love/Jesus was God."

Jesus is our first Prince!

Chapter Eight

Don't Quit

I don't know where you are right now in your marriage, but I want to encourage the faint-hearted and uphold the weak. Be patient with your spouse. Do not render evil for evil, but always pursue what is good.

This is God's will for you in Christ Jesus. Thank you for reading this far. Thank you for all you do when no one is watching. Thank you for staying married and being an example to the many who are watching you. You are a leader by example. I've opened up to you about my love adventure, and as you can see, it has not been an easy ride.

We have met with the realities of life, and the hoax of the "happily ever after" fairy tale. This chapter is for any one going through a tough time, and for those needing maintenance therapy.

Don't quit! There is hope when you stand on the promises of God, in Christ Jesus.

"The Lord is not slack concerning His promise, as some count slackness, but is long-suffering toward us, not willing that any should perish but that all should come to repentance."
- 2 Peter 3:9 NKJV

Have His promises as an anchor in your circumstances. You may have been praying and waiting on God for a change in your marriage. Don't quit! Continue to speak out loud His promises. Get a verse and stand on it. His covenant He will not break or change a Word He has spoken (Psalm 89:34). He is able to perform that which He has promised (Romans 4:21).

He is God and he changes not (Malachi 3:6)! He is always for you, and never against you. Rest assured that no matter the circumstances in your marriage, or its resulting condition, His love for you does not change. He wants to hold your hand, walking first through your love adventure with Him, and then through the journey with your spouse. Will you give Him the chance to lead you? It is your choice.

GOD IS ALWAYS FOR YOU, NEVER AGAINST YOU, AND HE NEVER CHANGES!

Be Encouraged, Dear Friend

I'm writing to encourage you about your marriage. I don't know exactly what you are going through, but what I do know is that you are hurting and trying to think of a solution. You got married to your spouse and had lots of expectations that were not realistic. You may have asked yourself this question, or are asking yourself right now, "How did I end up with this person?"

You see, every married person at some point finds themselves asking that exact question. And, if you are, I know you are hurting. I used to hurt like you. It's true, I did not know what to expect when I first got married. I really did not know my husband very well. However, you will never fully know a person enough to marry them.

Yes, the world has gotten it all wrong. Maybe you have heard of Bible stories about God telling His beloved who to marry. He was right in doing this. You don't just marry anyone, especially if you are born-again in Christ. It won't work unless you get a word from God.

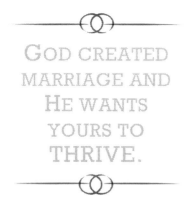

GOD CREATED MARRIAGE AND HE WANTS YOURS TO THRIVE.

This is what I want you to know: God loves marriage. He created and blessed the first marriage, and He wants you to have a great one. God wants to show the world what unconditional love is all about by displaying it in marriage. The vows you made to your spouse were witnessed by God. God signed as your witness because He wants to help your marriage thrive.

Isn't that what witnesses do? God stood with you, witnessing your vows to one another, and continues with you to help fulfill those vows. He spoke the truth when He said He will never leave you

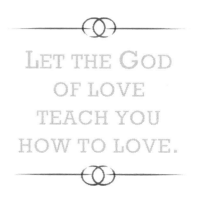

LET THE GOD OF LOVE TEACH YOU HOW TO LOVE.

nor forsake you. He is waiting for you to give Him a chance to be your counsel. You can't do marriage successfully on your own. Let the God of love teach you how to love in your situation.

Those feelings you are having are not love. You need to know that real love is not a feeling. Love is an action – a choice! Love is a Person, and His name is Jesus Christ. You take action by making the first choice of love by receiving His sacrifice of love and accepting Him as Lord and Savior. Then, you have to allow Him to be Lord of your marriage. It's a choice you must make. You choose to let Him live His life through you. You become lovable when you demonstrate the love of God living inside of you (as well as your spouse, which is only possible if Christ is in them) through your actions (1 John 4:7).

You may be wondering what has changed since you got married. It is your attitude toward your spouse because of hurt emotions. The only one person you can change in marriage is you. If you will change your attitude, and therefore your actions, toward your spouse, you will see your marriage change.

Change must come from the love of Christ within you. Work on yourself, partnering with the Holy Spirit, so that your spouse will be attracted to His unconditional love in you.

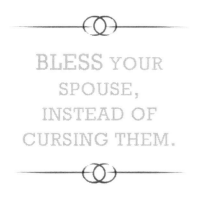

BLESS YOUR SPOUSE, INSTEAD OF CURSING THEM.

Bless your spouse instead of cursing them. You are one in Christ. Rebuking them is the same as rebuking yourself. You can rebuke the enemy in them by speaking directly to the enemy.

Why not try marriage with Jesus before you quit? Just ask The Holy Spirit to reveal His truth to you. Trust me, He will show up! He will instruct your heart and counsel you. He will bring the right people across your path, just as He did for me. You will rest in His everlasting arms of love.

You will realize that your spouse was not meant to make you happy. Happiness comes from the joy of the Lord. This joy from the Lord is what you need because it is eternal. You will serve your spouse from the overflow of eternal joy within your heart.

God wants your marriage to be a light of unconditional love in this dark world. For this to happen, you have to activate the voice of the Holy Spirit in your life. He speaks life and not death. It is impossible to love your spouse unconditionally without accepting the love of Christ.

"Beloved, let us love one another, for love is of God; and everyone who loves is born of God and knows God. He who does not love does not know God, for God is love. In this the love of God was manifested toward us, that God has sent His only begotten Son into the world, that we might live through Him. In this is love, not that we loved God, but that He loved us and sent His Son to be the propitiation for our sins. Beloved, if God so loved us, we also ought to love one another."
- I John 4:7-11 NKJV

Happiness Has a Name

I learned very quickly that my husband was not, and is not, the source of my joy and happiness. It is wrong thinking for anyone to expect a human being to keep them happy. Happiness starts in the heart. Get this clearly: no one else is responsible for your happiness. It is your choice to receive happiness.

NO ONE ELSE IS RESPONSIBLE FOR YOUR HAPPINESS.

Happiness is a constant lifestyle we receive from God because He spoke it over us and extended Himself to us. Making happiness a lifestyle depends on your knowledge of what this word really means. It is a gift that keeps giving. We are constantly unwrapping the gift to discover new things hidden by God just **for** us, but not **from** us. Let's do a word study before I continue.

Happiness, in the Hebrew language, is *esher*, which means blessedness, or happiness.

Happiness, in the Greek language, is *makarios*, which means happy, blessed, or to be envied.

To be blessed is when God extends His benefits

to you. That is, God extending His favor to you.

Are you getting something out of this? Happiness is basically a state of being which only comes when you reach out and receive God's favor that has already been extended to you. This should make others envy you. It's drinking from the fountain that never runs dry.

Has God not already favored us? This was God's original plan right from creation. That means you should constantly be in a state of happiness. The first words God spoke after He made man were, "Then God blessed them...(Gen 1:28)." Basically, He made man happy!

Why aren't people happy? There are a lot of disgruntled people walking around. When Adam sinned, things changed in the world. Sin came into the world and separated man from God.

This is the reason Jesus came into the world: to restore God's favor to us. Jesus is God's favor to man – He is happiness! Jesus is blessedness. God has extended all that He has to us by giving

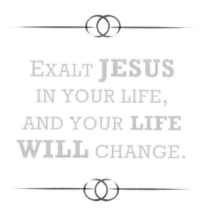

EXALT **JESUS** IN YOUR LIFE, AND YOUR **LIFE** **WILL** CHANGE.

us Jesus. We are back to the garden of Eden where everything was perfect. This is the Good News, my friends! Jesus is glad tidings. He is good news! I don't know about you, but good news makes me happy!

Exalt Jesus in your life, and your life will change – you will begin to see good! Focus on the finished work of Jesus to experience true joy.

Stop walking about looking for happiness in things and people. None of these will give you the happiness you are looking for. What you are missing is the revelation of Jesus in your life. Eternal happiness and blessedness can only be found in Jesus. Reach out and receive God's favor for your life today. Jesus is the missing puzzle piece you are looking for.

STOP LOOKING FOR HAPPINESS IN THINGS AND PEOPLE.

No job will give you happiness; no man or woman will give you happiness; your children won't give you happiness; your houses, cars, shoes, the latest clothes – you name it, nothing else will give you happiness. No matter what is happening around you or in your life, happiness will never leave, if you truly believe and trust in Christ Jesus. He was revealed to us by God. He came to us. God can't change a Word

www.victorynowmin.org

He has spoken. He would have to deny Himself to take happiness from us.

It is our choice to stay happy because God has already extended happiness toward you by giving you Jesus. Jesus is the fullness of God. Keep your focus on Jesus for he is the happiness you are seeking.

Oh! But why is there so much evil in the world? Because people have turned away from the truth!

Jesus is the truth. Jesus is what the world needs. The lack of revelation of God's truth is withholding happiness from us. When you receive happiness, compassion flows from you toward others who have not yet received this revelation. So, we don't get married to be happy! We receive happiness when we confess Jesus as Lord of our lives.

You Are Valuable

Can you give me a chance to speak into your life today? I feel in my spirit at this point, as I am writing, that someone needs to hear these words. So, this is the Father's heart for you today:

He is with you always; even in the fire! Maybe you have been hurt by a loved one, or rejected, abandoned, neglected, cheated on, abused, not appreciated, or slandered. Or maybe all kinds of evil words have been spoken over you. Maybe you can't stop crying in the dark, and it seems like no one cares about you. The good news is, none of these words define who you are.

NO EVIL WORDS SPOKEN OVER YOU DEFINE WHO YOU ARE.

Are you the single mom or dad working night and day, the married woman catering to her husband and children, the grandma bringing up grandchildren all alone, the grandma whom no one has visited, the widow missing her husband, the orphans struggling to get by, the barren woman trying to have children, the grandpa waiting for a call from his family, or the pastors working day and night without rest who are serving the flock without appreciation?

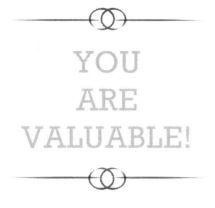

YOU ARE VALUABLE!

If this is you – you are valuable! Your Heavenly Father says, "Thank you for all you do." He values you. Rest in His love, for He cares about you. I want you to personalize this and say it out loud to your own ears. Replace "you are" with "I am," and "you" with "me":

"You are beautifully created in His image and likeness. You are marvelous, and there is no one else like you. You are blessed and highly favored amongst all others. You are fearfully and wonderfully made. You are a joint heir with Christ Jesus, seated in heavenly places with Him. You are a seed of Abraham and all his blessings belong to you. You have been set apart for God. You are anointed to do the work God has called you to do. You are perfect! You are the righteousness of God in Christ. You have the mind of Christ and you know all things. You are prosperous and successful.

You are wall to wall Holy Ghost! You are healed because His body was broken for you. You are victorious in Christ Jesus. You have been accepted into the family of the beloved. You are His beloved! You have been adopted and restored. You are forgiven and redeemed. You were bought with a price and are precious to God. You are a winner. You are complete in Christ. You are more than a conqueror.

You have been chosen and are a royal priesthood. You are treasured by the Father. You are His one special pearl. You are the head and not the tail; above and not below. You are an overcomer. You have been justified (just as if you never sinned). You are a qualified partaker with the saints. You were crucified with Christ.

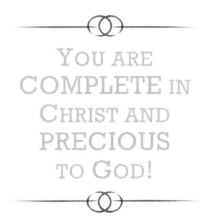

You Are COMPLETE in Christ and PRECIOUS to God!

You are dead to trespasses. You were buried with Christ. You were raised with Christ. You are alive with Christ! You are the elect of God! You reign with Christ!"

Glory be to God forever! Somebody shout, "Hallelujah!" Sing His praises with a loud voice!

This is how God sees you. This is who you are in Christ. See yourself as the Father sees you. Speak only what He speaks. You have been liberated and set free. You are in a Kingdom that cannot be moved. Be strong and be of good courage; He will never leave you nor forsake you! And all of God's children say Amen.

"Amen!!!"

Chapter Nine

Marriage in the Spirit

In chapter three, I had mentioned that God told me He was going to teach me what love is. Like most of us, I had the expectation that I would ultimately meet a godly man and marry. However, one thing was certain in my mind: I wanted to marry only once, and I needed discernment before I committed to my husband. I needed the peace of God like I never had before.

This is the reason I went to God for help. I had to go beyond my emotions and feelings in order to make the right choice. Unlike many, when I married my husband, I did not have all the butterflies in my stomach the way others describe as they are falling in love.

All I knew was that God told me to marry him, and I was confident that He put us together. One very important lesson I learned in this process is that relationship starts from a place of transparency and intimacy. For you to know anyone, you must intentionally create time for them and be open. In the movie, "Beauty and The Beast," the only reason Belle could fall in love with the Beast is because they spent time together. She figured out that the Beast was kind, and she was able to overlook her first impression of him, as well as what others were thinking.

RELATIONSHIP STARTS FROM A PLACE OF TRANSPARENCY AND INTIMACY.

This works in every relationship and is a principle of the Kingdom of God. Seed time and harvest time are spiritual laws. When you plant a seed, it needs time to grow, and you eventually know what you planted by the fruit it produces. I knew that I had reached a point in my marriage that only God could help. I had to be intentional about strengthening my relationship with the Prince of Peace. Sure enough, He gave me a revelation about marriage that has changed my life forever.

Before I explain this to you, let me ask you a question: if eternal life is knowing God, and our marriage with Christ is supposed to be a reflection of our be a reflection of our marriage here on earth, is knowing our spouse not also supposed to be a lifetime journey?

> MARRIAGE ON EARTH REFLECTS THE RELATIONSHIP OF CHRIST AND HIS BRIDE.

A Lifetime of Knowing Your Spouse

In John 17:3 Jesus said that eternal life is knowing God. Our marriage here on earth is a reflection of Christ and His bride.

Therefore, marriage should be a lifetime intentional commitment of knowing your spouse.

Marriage is a lifetime journey of

> MARRIAGE IS A LIFETIME JOURNEY OF KNOWING YOUR SPOUSE.

knowing your spouse! It does not take a day, or even a couple of years, to know someone fully. Statistics have shown that there are not many couples who make it through the first few years of marriage. By the second year of our marriage, it looked like it was going to be counted among these statistics.

Whatever happened to the happily ever after? It felt like a nightmare! Here I was, a new bride, yet a few days later I felt like I was trapped in a huge mess.

It takes time to build trust in a relationship! Just as your faith in God becomes stronger as you experience the Father's love, loving your spouse also takes time. In your Christian walk, your faith does not

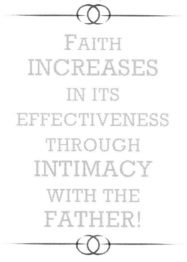

FAITH INCREASES IN ITS EFFECTIVENESS THROUGH INTIMACY WITH THE FATHER!

grow, but it increases in its effectiveness through intimacy with the Father. Jesus willingly laid down Himself for us because He trusted the Father to raise Him up from the dead. Jesus trusted the Father because He was with the father from the beginning and walked with Him. This baby, born like us, increased in wisdom as He spent intimate time with the Father. There is no other way to increase in wisdom than by spending intimate time with the Father.

We grow in the grace and knowledge of Jesus through intimacy with Him. The same applies in a marriage covenant.

You should be able to discern where your spouse's heart is before you get married. You can't compromise your faith in Christ when choosing the person you will marry.

WE GROW IN GRACE AND KNOWLEDGE THROUGH INTIMACY WITH GOD.

What was your reason for marriage? Was it because your parents forced you? Or, because you thought time was an issue? Did you marry because all of your friends were getting married? Did you see marriage as simply a way to get out of poverty? Were you tired of being single, or trying to run away from your parents? Did you meet a person you could not resist? Was it lust or manipulation?

Were you intentional about your choice? Even if the answer is, "No," if you are a believer there is no condemnation to those who are in Christ, who walk not according to the flesh, but according to the spirit (Romans 8:1).

Being intentional means that no one forced the choice on you. It was your free will; you are willing to do life with your spouse. So, there are no excuses.

Too often I hear people say, "I can't take this any longer. I did not know he (or she) was like this!" They are not alone. I was one of them! But, marriage is a lifetime of knowing your spouse; you never stop learning about each other. It is a lifetime commitment. So, don't use this as an excuse to escape. Stop running from yourself. If you are willing and obedient, then you will eat the good of your marriage (Isaiah 1:19). We inherit the promises of God through faith and patience (Hebrews 6:12). Being patient includes enduring through the challenges of marriage.

BEING PATIENT INCLUDES ENDURING THROUGH THE CHALLENGES OF MARRIAGE.

Again, knowing your spouse takes time, experience, and endurance. First and foremost, knowing someone starts from a place of intimacy with the Father. If you truly desire a successful marriage, relationship with the Prince of Peace is the key. It will get you pregnant with the knowledge of how to love and trust your spouse; and you will gain wisdom, and so much in-sight, into having a wonderful marriage.

Unfortunately, many get married thinking that they already fully know their spouse. This is the reason many marriages don't last very long. You have to be intentional about the relationship, but also aware that you can't have a successful marriage in the flesh alone. It takes your entire being – spirit, soul and body. It can't only be in the body, or even just the body and the soul. Marriage starts in your spirit. It is your spirit that is supposed to be leading your soul and body.

In marriage, you are joined in spirit. We are joined with Christ through our spirits. You may be wondering what I mean by that, but keep reading, I will explain this a little later!

LIKE WITH JESUS, WE ARE JOINED IN SPIRIT WITH OUR SPOUSES.

If the spirits of both spouses are not connected as one, you are in for a real war. Although in the physical realm opposites attract, in the spirit realm opposites do not attract, they repel each other. This is why the Bible says not to be unequally yoked with an unbeliever in marriage (1 Corinthians 6:14). No matter how physically attractive a man (or woman) is, if their spirit is not one with Christ you should not marry them.

This is the reason why I said marriage must be intentional. This is the most important factor in choosing a spouse, but unfortunately many people get married before they figure this out. The good news is, with Jesus on your side you are an overcomer!

This is why Jesus came: to separate light from darkness. He has deposited His spirit within us and He teaches us all things. His perfect love for us casts out all fear and is the bond of perfection (Genesis 1:4, John 14:26, 1 John 4:18, Colossians 3:14).

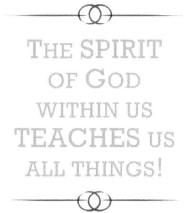

THE SPIRIT OF GOD WITHIN US TEACHES US ALL THINGS!

Let His light shine through you. Light came into the world when Jesus was born. God was intentional when He sent Jesus into the world. Be intentional in your intimacy with God.

When my husband and I got connected in the spirit, our ability to discern was much better. The Holy Spirit would speak something to me and confirm the same thing to him. I did not have to try to convince my husband about things. All I had to do was tell the Holy Spirit to tell him also. This is a very powerful aspect of marriage we need to tap into – unity with the Holy Spirit.

www.victorynowmin.org

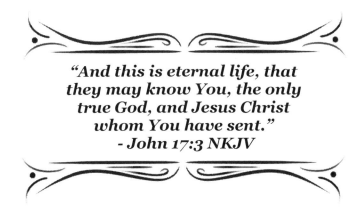

*"And this is eternal life, that
they may know You, the only
true God, and Jesus Christ
whom You have sent."*
- John 17:3 NKJV

Word Study

What is the meaning of the word "know?" Merriam Webster dictionary has it defined as, "to have direct cognition, to have practical understanding, to discern, to recognize, to have experience, to be aware of the truth, to have sexual intercourse."

In Greek, "know" is the word *ginosko*, which means to know through experience.

Therefore, we can only know God through our experience with Him. This can be possible only through personal relationship; the more we spend time with Him, the more we will know Him.

It works the same way in relationship with our spouses. And, guess what? Knowing God more intimately will get you pregnant with an inexplicable desire for a better, deeper relationship in your marriage. Knowing starts from a place of intimacy.

Knowing keeps us at rest with God as well as with our spouses. Knowing means transparency, both with God and with your spouse. Knowing takes silencing all other voices yet being sensitive to His voice. Knowing requires diligence in seeking Him with all your heart, so that you will find Him (Jeremiah 29:13). You can't just passively know God. That is why a double-minded man cannot receive from Him (James 1:7).

It is the same with our spouses. You cannot passively be in a relationship with your spouse. Passivity breeds doubt; a double-minded person is unstable in all his ways. Knowing takes partnership, contributory help, participation and sharing with one another all that you own.

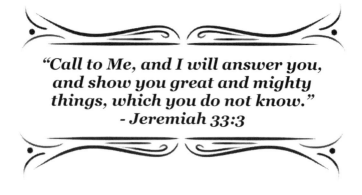

"Call to Me, and I will answer you, and show you great and mighty things, which you do not know."
- Jeremiah 33:3

 www.victorynowmin.org

Knowing is being in communion and fellowship with one another.

"Grace and peace be multiplied to you in the knowledge of God and of Jesus our Lord, as His divine power has given to us all things that pertain to life and godliness, through the knowledge of Him who called us by glory and virtue, by which have been given to us exceedingly great and precious promises, that through these you may be partakers of the divine nature, having escaped the corruption that is in the world through lust."
- 2 Peter 1:2-4 NKJV

My Revelation from God

In the summer of 2015, after my dad's passing, I was reflecting on how God used his letter to me to reveal so many truths regarding marriage. I was thanking God for his life, what a special man he was and what a gift he had been to me. As I sat on my living room couch, wondering how my life would be without my dad's physical presence here on earth, the Holy Spirit began to speak to me. It was clear that I was having a moment with God. He asked me two questions:

"Do you know why a threefold cord cannot be easily broken (Ecclesiastes 4:12)?"

"Do you know why I said not to be unequally yoked together with an unbeliever (2 Corinthians 6:14)?"

Well, I opened my Bible to read these scriptures again, to see if I missed something. So, I told the Holy Spirit to teach me what they meant.

I said, "You are the teacher and I am your student." He reminded me that we are made of spirit, soul and body.

Body – this is what we see in the mirror, our flesh.

Soul – the mind, will and emotions. This is the part of us that gets hurt when negative words are spoken to us. It contains all the philosophies of the world. The counsel of the ungodly is learned here!

Spirit – every human is born with a dead spirit because of the sin nature. From birth, man's spirit is in complete darkness with no life in it. Man lost the ability to see spiritually when Adam sinned. That is why they realized they were naked after they ate of the tree of the knowledge of good and evil (Genesis 3:7).

Yet, man was created as a spirit being. All we see today, with our eyes, comes from what we don't physically see.

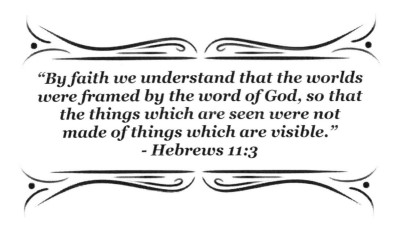

"By faith we understand that the worlds were framed by the word of God, so that the things which are seen were not made of things which are visible."
- Hebrews 11:3

The spirit world is, in reality, more dominant than the physical realm. We don't see air, but we breathe it. We don't see Wi-Fi, but we enter codes and get connected. We don't see radio waves, but we listen to the radio.

Before you become born-again, your spirit is susceptible to evil spirits because it is empty and in total darkness. However, once a person becomes born-again, God creates a new spirit in them. 2 Corinthians 5:17 says that if any man is in Christ, he is a new creation, that old things have passed away and all things have been made new. This now becomes your "new man," in Christ.

Sons of God are led by the Spirit of God. Now, since we were born in the flesh spiritually dead, our new spirit in Christ is the younger part of our being.

Do you remember the story of Esau and Jacob? While Rebekah was pregnant, the Bible says that the two boys "struggled" with one another in the womb.

So, she inquired of the Lord:

"And the Lord said to her:
Two nations are in your womb,
Two peoples shall be separated from
your body;
One people shall be stronger than the
other, And the older shall serve the
younger."

Just like Jacob, who is the younger, would rule over the older twin, Esau, our new spirit, which is younger, must rule over our body and soul, who are the older parts of our beings. Our new man is as perfect as Jesus is. This is the reason why perfect God has made His dwelling in all who are born by the Spirit of God.

In Christ, our spirits are perfect, mature, complete, elevated, re-created, righteous, holy and pure. All life and light originate from our born-again spirits, and this is the part of us that cannot sin (1 John 3:9). Our spirits in Christ should flow through our souls and bodies. Our spirits cannot be sick, and God communicates to us through our spirits. This is where the life of God flows through and into us. The Bible is our spiritual mirror, to show us our true identity in Christ – what we look like spiritually. This is the reason we have to renew our minds – our souls – with God's Word. We need to know His thoughts and perspective of us.

OUR SPIRITS CANNOT BE SICK, AND GOD SPEAKS TO US THROUGH OUR SPIRITS.

Well, how does this relate to marriage? At the moment of our salvation, we are joined in marriage to Christ. We are then reconciled to God in Christ. The Holy Spirt comes and resides in us. We are now in the light.

Now, when you marry another believer, the life of Christ flows through both of you. Your union becomes united by the Spirit of God, who is our bond of perfection. In the spirit realm, like spirits attract.

Now, when a born-again believer marries an un-believer, they are unequally yoked. This creates a problem. The law of physical attraction says opposites attract; that is why a man marries a woman. Only a sperm and an egg can produce another human. This is how God made it to be and no one can change this.

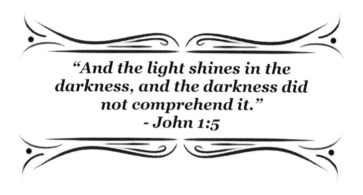

"And the light shines in the darkness, and the darkness did not comprehend it."
- John 1:5

The difference in the spirit realm is that light has already overpowered darkness. Darkness must disappear once light appears. Thus, opposites in the spirit realm will repel each other. This is the primary reason why many marriages are at war and they don't know why. The spirit of God can't unite two partners when they are unequally yoked. The spirit of God that is in the believer cannot unite with the spirit of darkness that is in the unbeliever.

Their marriage is merely in the flesh, and flesh

will fail you. The three-fold cord is not present; there-fore, the marriage is not perfected in the spirit. I hope this brings some understanding about marriage in the spirit. Christ is our bond of perfection and only like spirits can be united in Christ.

This is why it is very important to know who you marry and is the same reason that God told the chil-dren of Israel not to marry from other nations that did not believe in the One true God. When you intention-ally marry outside of your faith, your spouse becomes a thorn in your flesh. God is telling us today not to be unequally yoked together with unbelievers.

"Nor shall you make marriages with them. You shall not give your daughter to their son, nor take their daughter for your son. For they will turn your sons away from following Me, to serve other gods..."
- Deuteronomy 7:3-4 NKJV

The old covenant stories were told so we could learn from them. We bring destruction to ourselves when we rebel against God's promises and deny His wisdom.

You may be asking, "What if I did not know about this and I married an unbeliever?"

DON'T LET YOUR HEART CONDEMN YOU. THE SPIRIT OF GOD DOES NOT CONDEMN!

My friend, you are not the first to ask this question. Do not let your heart condemn you. The Spirit of God does not condemn. God is greater than your heart.

Paul wrote about this subject to the church of Corinth. Read 1 Corinthians 7:10-16, but I want to specifically highlight verse 14. It reads:

> *"For the unbelieving husband is sanctified by the wife, and the unbelieving wife is sanctified by the husband; otherwise your children would be unclean, but now they are holy."*

1 Peter 3:1-2 also brings light regarding this situation:

> *"Wives, in the same way submit yourselves to your own husbands so that, if any of them do not believe the word, they may be won over without words by the behavior of their wives, when they see the purity and reverence of your lives."*

Basically, the advice is to not divorce an unbelieving spouse if they don't want to leave you. Instead, allow your experience with God to draw them to Christ. Agree with God's Word over their lives and let the Holy Spirit do the work in their hearts.

Chapter Ten

Understanding Agape Love

I t was in October of 2016 that the Holy Spirit spelled out the meaning of love to me for the first time. That year was very challenging regarding my family. Many close to me were going through tough times in their marriages. I remember asking God, "What is going on?" It was devastating for me to see my loved ones hurting. I was hurting as if I was directly involved.

I woke up one morning with this scripture playing over and over in my heart: ***"Now hope does not disappoint, because the love of God has been***

poured out in our hearts by the Holy Spirit who was given to us" (Romans 5:5 NKJV).

So, I asked the Lord the meaning of this scripture and He explained, **"Etonde, what you are experiencing is compassion because you love your family members. When they hurt, I also hurt. My love has been poured out in you, and you are able to hurt for them because you have found the truth. When My children hurt, compassion flows through you toward them. Compassion reaches out to all who are hurting. I AM close to the broken hearted."**

Words cannot explain to you how I felt that morning. The tangible presence of God toward the broken hearted manifested itself through me.

THE TANGIBLE COMPASSION OF GOD TOWARD THE BROKEN HEARTED IS IN ME.

You see, *agape* love never existed until Jesus came. We can see what agape love does when we look at the ministry of Jesus Christ. He always reached out to the lost and hurting; He healed all who were sick; He fed the hungry; He made a way when there seemed to be no way. Agape love has a Name. He is the second person of the Trinity, and His Name is Jesus Christ. Agape is sacrificial love for one's friend; He laid down His life for us all.

Agape love is a gift given from God to His children. For you to receive the gift you must first accept the giver, Jesus Christ. Once you receive the gift, God plants His seed in you.

"having been born again, not of corruptible seed but incorruptible, through the word of God which lives and abides forever,"
- 1 Peter 1:23

You become the temple of the Living God because you are righteous, just as Jesus is. The gift you received must be revealed by the Spirit of Truth. Therefore, the agape love to which I have been referring must be revealed through fellowship with the Father.

I want to remind you of Jeremiah 33:3, which says, ***"Call to Me and I will answer you, and show you great and mighty things, which you do not***

know." Agape love is present with us always. Jesus Christ promised not to leave us as orphans. So, He sent us the same Spirit He had while He was on Earth – The Holy Spirit!

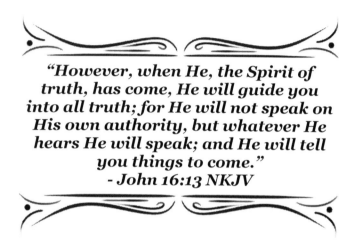

"However, when He, the Spirit of truth, has come, He will guide you into all truth; for He will not speak on His own authority, but whatever He hears He will speak; and He will tell you things to come."
- John 16:13 NKJV

Sons of God are led by the Spirit of God that has been poured out in their hearts. That morning, while brushing my teeth and meditating, I had a vision.

The Holy Spirit spelled out L-O-V-E to me. He said, **"Do you know what the letters stand for? Every letter has a meaning of its own. I picked them out to show my children that agape is sacrificial love. The letters say who I AM, what I did, and who you are in Christ. Therein lies your victory."**

I stood in front of my mirror, dumbfounded by what had just happened.

This is what I saw:

L = Living, Life, Light, Liberty
O = Overcame, Overcomer
V = Victorious, Victory
E = Everlasting, Eternal

I AM

The Living One; I give Life; I AM the Light of the world. Where the Spirit of the Lord is, there is Liberty. I came to proclaim Liberty to the captives; to set at Liberty those who are oppressed.

I Overcame the enemy and you are an Overcomer in Christ.

I AM Victorious, and your Victory is in Christ.

I AM Everlasting and Eternal life is knowing Me.

This is Agape Love spelled out and given to me in a vision. It concluded my search for answers to the question, "Is happily ever after a reality or a hoax?" He gave me a message for my ministry here on earth.

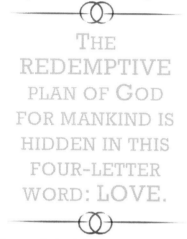

THE REDEMPTIVE PLAN OF GOD FOR MANKIND IS HIDDEN IN THIS FOUR-LETTER WORD: LOVE.

Just like the letter from my dad said, "Marriage is a living thing."

I had known all these words sepa-rately, but I had never seen them spelled out this way. This is a whole teaching on its own, so I won't even try to explain this further. However, it is apparent that the redemptive plan of God for mankind is hidden in this four-letter word: LOVE.

Agape love does not fail, even if you have failed in your marriage. God does not fail and will never fail. Love is about the Living God and His reconciling the world back to Himself, not feelings derived from lust. When you can truly see this, you will never see LOVE the same way again. This is a new picture the Father will paint in your mind.

There is no love in marriage apart from the love of God. The doctrines of man, and the philosophies of this world, might have destroyed the foundation of

LOVE, but God does not change. Love never fails because all life is from Him.

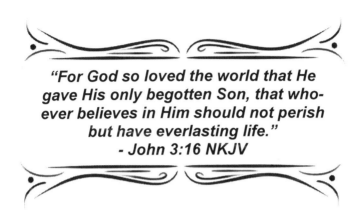

"For God so loved the world that He gave His only begotten Son, that whoever believes in Him should not perish but have everlasting life."
- John 3:16 NKJV

Understanding agape love is key to living happily ever after in your marriage. Even when trials and tribulations come your way, you will triumph over them when you magnify Jesus (love manifested in the flesh) over your trials. If agape love is not understood, happily after ever will remain a hoax. The reason for the high divorce rates in the world and amongst Christians is the lack of knowledge of **Agape Love**.

It was after receiving this revelation that my husband and I started the LOVE SEMINAR. God put it in my heart to share this truth to all who are married or ever will be married. He gave me His word in 2007, **"I will teach you what LOVE is."** He hid this revelation for me, not from me. Our desire is to bring to light

REST IN
GOD'S LOVE
FOR YOU
AND TEACH
OTHERS TO
DO THE
SAME!

the original plan of God for marriage: to rest in His love for us, and to teach others to do the same.

Love has already been accomplished. Yes! Love was done when Jesus became the Lamb of God that was sacrificially slain to reconcile the world back to the Father. All we need is to let Him manifest His life through us as we fellowship with the Father. Remember, the last letter of LOVE is E. Love is everlasting, and eternal life is knowing God and Jesus Christ whom God sent.

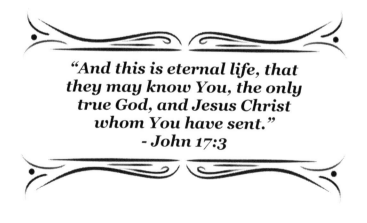

"And this is eternal life, that they may know You, the only true God, and Jesus Christ whom You have sent."
- John 17:3

www.victorynowmin.org

Isn't our purpose here on Earth to be conformed into the image of the Son of God? Isn't the love of God in Christ Jesus (Romans 8:29)? Can I now boldly and confidently say that sustaining Love for marriages is found only in the Son of God? Let God be true and every man a liar (Romans 3:4)!

Living happily ever after depends on you realizing that the love the world is seeking is only found in Christ Jesus. Apart from this revelation, happily ever after will remain a hoax.

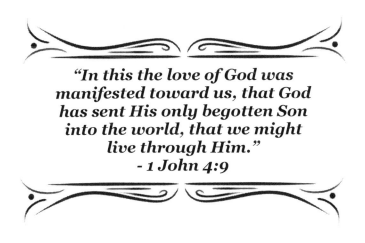

"In this the love of God was manifested toward us, that God has sent His only begotten Son into the world, that we might live through Him."
- 1 John 4:9

Conclusion

Ipray that, in our walk through my journey of meeting my Prince Charming, you have found answers to many of the questions we had regarding marriage. We discovered that people are searching for love in places where it cannot be found, and that the only source of true love comes from God.

I expressed to you that if there is trouble in your marriage, do not hesitate to seek help. And, you don't have to wait for a crisis to do so! Find a few Titus 2 women to help you in your journey. They are a gift to be valued highly!

Successful marriages take both spouses approaching it intentionally and in unity. However, that unity can begin with only one willing spouse, in cooperation with the Holy Spirit, stepping out in obedience. The one spouse in submission to God can be the open door to hearts being mended. It begins with intimate fellowship with God individually and ends with serving one another the way Christ served us.

We must know that our marriages, and families, are at war, but that our war is not with one another – it is with the thief who comes to steal, kill and destroy! We must be wise, use our authority over him, and be vigilant in not allowing strife to have a foothold in our homes. Unity is vital to victory!

God loves you, and He wants your marriage to succeed. Even in the midst of heartache, He is there to comfort, heal and restore. And just like Jesus was the firstborn seed that God planted to reap the harvest of the family of God, in us, the love that we plant as a seed in our homes will reap a harvest as well!

We learned that many marriages fail because people look to other people for happiness, and that can never meet the need. Our joy can only be found in our relationship with Christ.

Love was completed when God sent Jesus to die on the cross for us. Now, out of our intimacy with Him, we can have true fellowship with one another.

www.victorynowmin.org

We can love our spouses the way that God has loved us, not in our own strength, but out of His love that is present on the inside of us. We can have victory in our marriages because of Him!

Prayers

Some of you may be dealing with the heartbreak of having a spouse who has been, or even still is, unfaithful. This prayer is for spouses who are cheating. The best thing that you can do for an unfaithful husband, or wife, is to pray for them.

Prayer for an Unfaithful Spouse from Hosea 2:6-7

"Behold,

The Lord will hedge up <u>(your spouse's name)</u>'s way with thorns, and wall him/her in, so that _____ cannot find his/her paths. He/she will chase his/her lovers, but will not overtake them; Yes, he/she will seek them, but not find them. Then he/she will say, "I will go and return to my first spouse, <u>(your name)</u>, For then it was better for me than now."

Prayer for Marriages

I pray for those married people reading this right now. I come into agreement with you concerning your heart's desire for your marriage. Thank You, Holy Spirit for ministering Your truth to everyone reading this right now. You are our counsellor and help. Thank You, Lord for instructing our hearts. Thank You, Holy Father, for always hearing us when we pray. Thank You, Jesus that before we call, You answer, and while we are still speaking You hear us. Thank You, Lord that what we behold and speak of our marriage shall come to pass.

I speak life and divine protection over you household, in Jesus' Name. As you seek the Lord diligently, He will be found by you. The Lord will show you deep secrets of the heart you did not know as you continue seeking to know the truth. The favor of the Lord is a shield over your family. Goodness and mercy shall follow you all the days of your life. You shall prosper in all you do. Your barns will overflow, and you will be a lender to many and shall not borrow. The blessing of the Lord will overtake you. The Lord will withhold no good thing from you, and you shall lack nothing. He shall cause you to inherit wealth and fill your bank accounts to establish His kingdom on Earth because you have put your trust in Him.

I speak healing over your family in Jesus' Name. Your health is being restored right now as you always exalt Jesus over your condition. The body of Jesus was broken for your healing. Healing is the children's bread and belongs to you. Thank You, Father for the blood of Jesus shed for us. I speak death to ovarian cysts and cancers causing infertility in Jesus' Name. Let God's Word be true and exalted above every medical diagnosis. For all those believing to get pregnant: healthy children will be conceived in your wombs. The fruit of your womb is blessed because children are gift from the Lord. There shall be no miscarriage or barrenness in your house in Jesus' Name.

Your children shall be taught in the Way of the Lord. In righteousness they shall be established. No one will be able be stand against you and your children all the days of your life. Your sons will be like plants grown up in their youth and your daughters will be like pillars sculptured in palace style; for the Lord will pour out His Spirit upon them and make His Word known to them. They shall be a light in this dark world and world changers for Jesus.

I pray peace over your family and the decisions you make. May the peace of God always lead you in all you do. God is doing a new thing in your family this season in Jesus' Name. It shall spring forth and you shall know it. He is making rivers in the dry places of your marriage. Continue to drink from the fountain that never runs dry. It is God's desire to fill you up, reach out and drink. Come all who are thirsty and drink the new wine and fresh milk for free. Come eat from the bread of life, all who have no money. Stop spending your money in things that don't satisfy; delight your soul in the abundance found in Christ Jesus alone.

Your family shall be far from oppression and you shall not live in fear for the Lord is your confidence. Whoever comes against you shall fall for your sake. No weapon formed against your marriage shall prosper, and every tongue that speaks against your marriage in judgement is condemned. God wants your marriage to be a reflection of His love for us (Christ and His Church). This is your heritage as children of God as you stand on the promises of God. Happy are the marriages whose God is the Lord! You shall live to a ripe old age and see your children's children in Jesus' Name! His covenant He will not break, nor change a word He has spoken. Amen!

www.victorynowmin.org

Daily Confession

I am the Righteousness of God in Christ.
I have been made Holy by Christ.
I am Anointed.
I have been Sanctified.
I am Blessed to be a blessing.
I have Favor with God.
I have Favor with Man.
I have Good understanding.
I have the mind of Christ.
I am Peaceful.
I have been Chosen and Adopted.
I am Royalty.
I am seated in Heavenly places with Christ.
I am Beautiful and whole.
I am Healed.
I am the Head and not the tail.
I am Above and not below.
No plague shall come near my dwelling.
No weapon formed against me shall prosper.
I shall Live to a ripe old age.
I am not afraid because Jesus is with me always.
I am His dwelling place.
I am Prosperous in every area of life.
Whatever I touch shall Prosper.
As Jesus is, so I am in this world.
Glory be to God forever!!!

Salvation Prayer

If you have never entered into fellowship with my Heavenly Father, through faith in His Son, Jesus, I invite you to do so right now! If there is any doubt in your heart about this decision, it does not hurt to confess Him as Lord and Savior. He is waiting for you to join His family. God's Word promises in Romans 10:9-10,13, **"That if thou shalt confess with thy mouth the Lord Jesus, and shalt believe in thine heart that God hath raised him from the dead, thou shalt be saved. For with the heart man believeth unto righteousness; and with the mouth confession is made unto salvation.... For whosoever shall call upon the name of the Lord shall be saved."**

By His grace, God has already done everything to provide salvation for you. Your part is simply to believe and receive. Pray this out loud:

"Jesus, I confess that You are my Lord and Savior. I believe in my heart that God raised You from the dead. By faith in Your Word, I receive salvation now. Thank You for saving me!"

If you just prayed that prayer for the first time, welcome into the family of God! The Kingdom of Heaven is rejoicing right now because of your choice.

Receive the Holy Spirit

I also encourage you to ask the Father to give you the gift of the Holy Spirit. This is called the baptism of the Holy Spirit. If you are in doubt about this, just ask God to reveal himself to you.

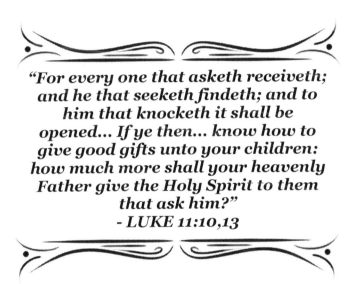

"For every one that asketh receiveth; and he that seeketh findeth; and to him that knocketh it shall be opened... If ye then... know how to give good gifts unto your children: how much more shall your heavenly Father give the Holy Spirit to them that ask him?"
- LUKE 11:10,13

As God's child, your loving Heavenly Father wants to give you the supernatural power you need to live this new life in victory.

All you need to do is ask, believe, and receive! To receive the baptism of the Holy Spirit, with the evidence of speaking in tongues, pray this prayer:

"Father, I recognize my need for Your power in order to live this new life. Please fill me with Your Holy Spirit. By faith, I receive Him right now! Thank You for baptizing me. Holy Spirit, You are welcome in my life."

Congratulations, friend! Now you're filled with God's supernatural power. You will find that some syllables, from a heavenly language you don't recognize, will rise up from your belly to your mouth (1 Corinthians 14:14). As you speak them out loud by faith, you're releasing God's power from within and building yourself up in the Spirit (1 Corinthians 14:4). You can do this whenever and wherever you like.

It doesn't really matter whether you **felt** anything or not when you prayed to receive the Lord's salvation and the baptism of His Spirit. If you believed in your heart that you received, then God's Word promises that you did!

God always honors His Word; believe it!

"Therefore, I say unto you, What things soever ye desire, when ye pray, believe that ye receive them, and ye shall have them"
- Mark 11:24

If you would like to contact us, please visit our website:

www.victorynowmin.org

Made in the USA
Columbia, SC
21 July 2018